FACES OF HMS ROYAL OAK

FACES OF HMS ROYAL OAK
THE 'MIGHTY OAK' DISASTER AT SCAPA FLOW

Dilip Sarkar MBE FRHistS

FRONTLINE
BOOKS

FACES OF HMS ROYAL OAK
The 'Mighty Oak' Disaster at Scapa Flow

First published in Great Britain in 2023 by

Frontline Books
An imprint of
Pen & Sword Books Ltd
Yorkshire – Philadelphia

Copyright © Dilip Sarkar, 2023

ISBN 978 1 39906 232 9

The right of Dilip Sarkar to be identified as Author of this work has been asserted by him in accordance with the Copyright, Designs and Patents Act 1988.

A CIP catalogue record for this book is available from the British Library.

All rights reserved. No part of this book may be reproduced or transmitted in any form or by any means, electronic or mechanical including photocopying, recording or by any information storage and retrieval system, without permission from the Publisher in writing.

Typeset by SJmagic DESIGN SERVICES, India.

Printed and bound in the UK by CPI Group (UK) Ltd.

Pen & Sword Books Limited incorporates the imprints of Atlas, Archaeology, Aviation, Discovery, Family History, Fiction, History, Maritime, Military, Military Classics, Politics, Select, Transport, True Crime, Air World, Frontline Publishing, Leo Cooper, Remember When, Seaforth Publishing, The Praetorian Press, Wharncliffe Local History, Wharncliffe Transport, Wharncliffe True Crime and White Owl.

For a complete list of Pen & Sword titles please contact

PEN & SWORD BOOKS LIMITED
George House, Units 12 & 13, Beevor Street, Off Pontefract Road,
Barnsley, South Yorkshire, S71 1HN, England
E-mail: enquiries@pen-and-sword.co.uk
Website: www.pen-and-sword.co.uk

or
PEN AND SWORD BOOKS
1950 Lawrence Rd, Havertown, PA 19083, USA
E-mail: uspen-and-sword@casematepublishers.com
Website: www.penandswordbooks.com

Contents

Foreword by the HMS Royal Oak Association vi

Part I   'The Mighty Oak' and 'The Boldest of Bold Enterprises' 1

Part II   The Photographs 75

Acknowledgements 202

Bibliography 204

Other Books by Dilip Sarkar MBE, FRHistS 206

Foreword

By the HMS Royal Oak Association

It is now over eighty-three years since the loss of HMS *Royal Oak* and 835 men and boys – well over half of her crew – as the result of enemy action. The tragedy and the number of casualties at such an early stage of the Second World War shocked the nation, especially given that the sinking occurred in what was considered to be the impregnable anchorage of Scapa Flow. The impact was particularly sharp in Portsmouth, HMS *Royal Oak's* home port, and the surrounding areas from where many of the crew either originated or lived. Countless families were left devastated as widows contemplated how to survive the war and beyond and children grew up deprived of their fathers. Sadly, all of the survivors of the sinking have 'crossed the bar', at least to the best of our knowledge. However, as some of those children deprived of their fathers now become more advanced in years and stories are passed down to the next generations, the tragic loss still reverberates today within families connected to HMS *Royal Oak*.

The HMS *Royal Oak* Association – established originally by survivors – is recognised by the Royal Navy as the body which represents the families of the crew of HMS *Royal Oak*. Its aim is to ensure that the memory of the ship and her crew is maintained and to act as a focal point for those with a connection to the vessel. It is proud to have those responsibilities. The Association works with the Royal Navy and other long standing friends and connections to hold annual services of remembrance in Portsmouth and at Scapa Flow on or around the anniversary of the loss: 14 October. It has also arranged for memorials at St Ann's Church in HM Naval Base in Portsmouth, the National Memorial Arboretum and at Scapa Flow. At the time of writing, discussions are progressing with the relevant authorities to install a permanent memorial to HMS *Royal Oak* at the entrance to HM Naval Base in Portsmouth to further enhance the connection to her home port. The Association would not have met its aims without the generosity and support of Association members and friends over many years in the form of donations as well as collections at the services of remembrance in Portsmouth.

The activities of the HMS *Royal Oak* Association and the memorials it has created ensure that the memory of the ship and her crew is maintained. They also act as a reminder for future generations of the sacrifices made by others in the struggle for freedom and of the devastation caused by conflict.

We are grateful to Dilip Sarkar for his continued interest in our ship and its story, and the support of his publisher, Pen and Sword. Whilst many accounts of the loss of HMS *Royal Oak* have been produced, Dilip's latest book focuses on the human aspect of the disaster – which is brought to life by unique photographs, providing moving insights into the lives of the crew of HMS *Royal Oak*, personalising the stark detail of the long casualty list.

The photographs, personal stories and items specific to individuals and families have largely been provided by Association members and friends. The cooperation of all involved is greatly appreciated, as this goes a long way to sharing this tragic story widely and maintaining the currency of the casualties memory.

Gareth Derbyshire
Honorary Secretary, HMS Royal Oak Association
December 2022

Part I

'The Mighty Oak' and 'The Boldest of Bold Enterprises'

'The Mighty Oak' and 'The Boldest of Bold Enterprises'

Without doubt, notwithstanding the ship's ultimately tragic end, HMS *Royal Oak* harks back to the time when Britannia ruled the waves.

A Revenge class battleship of 30,450 tons, this great ship was 620 ft, 7 in long, with a beam of 88 ft 6 in. Her eighteen Yarrow boilers powered four shafts and two steam turbines, making the ship capable of 22 knots (25 mph), with a maximum range of 7,000 nautical miles. Laid down at Devonport Royal Dockyard at a cost of £2,468,269 on 15 January 1915, *Royal Oak* was launched on 17 November 1914 and Commissioned on 1 May 1916. The ship's name was taken from the fabled oak in which King Charles II hid after his defeat at the Battle of Worcester in 1651, although more commonly she was known as 'The Mighty Oak'. The eighth ship so named, *Royal Oak*'s was comprised of four twin 15-inch guns, each pair accommodated in armour plated turrets, fourteen single 6-inch guns, two single 3-inch anti-aircraft guns and four 21-inch torpedo tubes.

Upon completion and commission, *Royal Oak* joined the Third Division of the Fourth Battle Squadron of the Grand Fleet, and was initially commanded by Captain Crawford Maclachlan. The ship would take part in the First World War's most significant naval engagement, the Battle of Jutland, fought off the Danish coast between 31 May and 1 June 1916 between the British Grand Fleet and German High Seas Fleet. During this titanic clash, *Royal Oak*'s gunners scored hits on the enemy ships *Wiesbaden*, *Derfflinger* and *Seydlitz*. Indeed, during the battle *Royal Oak* fired thirty-eight rounds from her 15-inch guns and a further eighty-four from her lesser weapons. Although straddled by a salvo fired by *Wiesbaden*, *Royal Oak* was undamaged.

After the First World War, *Royal Oak*'s anti-aircraft defences were upgraded and increased between 1922 and 1924, the 3-inch guns replaced by a pair of 102mm Mk V Anti-Aircraft (AA) guns. Rangefinders were also fitted and below the waterline anti-torpedo bulges were added – these air-filled pockets providing a cushion to absorb a torpedo explosion, thereby reducing damage – although this increased beam reduced the ship's speed. Originally, the ship's company numbered 909 men, but as various refits over the years added new equipment, requiring more manpower, this figure had increased by 1927 to 1,188. A further, major re-fit followed in 1934–36, which saw deck armour increased over the engine room and magazine, the addition of multiple 'pom-pom' and other AA guns, changes to torpedo tubes and construction of a radio direction finding (radar) office. In 1937, *Royal Oak* was deployed to patrol the Iberian Peninsula during the Spanish Civil War and survived – undamaged – an ill-advised aerial attack by the Republicans, who were forced to apologise. A month later, five of *Royal Oak*'s crew, including the Captain, T.B. Drew, were injured when the ship was accidentally hit by Republican AA gunners fighting off a Nationalist air attack. By 1938, *Royal Oak* had returned to the Home Fleet and took up station as the Portsmouth-based Second Battle Squadron's flagship. By that time, however, *Royal Oak* was past her prime, given developments in Germany, since the Nazis came to power in 1933. For example, on 1 July 1936, the German battleship *Bismarck* was laid down in Hamburg, with greater speed, range and heavier armament. Obsolete, *Royal Oak* was paid off in December 1938, but with another war with Germany looming large, she was recommissioned in June 1939. It was originally intended, after working up in the Channel, to send *Royal Oak* on a long tour of the Mediterranean, but as tension mounted and war became imminent, she was deployed to Scapa Flow in the Orkneys, where 'The Mighty Oak' was at anchor that fateful day, 3 September 1939, when Britain and France declared war on Nazi Germany.

Scapa Flow, that famous Royal Naval anchorage, was a name hated in Germany. At the end of the First World War, the German High Seas Fleet was ordered to surrender to the British and be interned there. Over the following months, thousands of German sailors were repatriated, leaving caretaker crews aboard each of the seventy-four interned ships. These men were not allowed ashore, nor any contact with Orcadians or British seamen. On Midsummer Day 1919, the German commander, Admiral von Reuter, signaled from the cruiser *Emden* that the fleet was to be scuttled. So it was that this once proud Fleet settled on the bottom of Scapa Flow in what was a further humiliation for Germany, now smarting from the draconian restrictions and reparations imposed by the Versailles Peace Treaty. Under the provisions of this hated *Diktat*, Germany's military was massively reduced, its air force prohibited, as were submarines. Nonetheless, after Hitler came to power and began denouncing Versailles, the U-boat fleet was reconstructed – secretly at first until, totally confident following years of appeasement, Hitler advised Britain that the tonnage of the 129 U-boats now on charge equalled the tonnage of the Royal Navy's submarine fleet.

A former First World War U-boat veteran was commanding the 1st U-Boat Flotilla by 1939; *Kommodore* Karl Dönitz began building the foundation blocks of his personal vision: that one day Germany would have 300 U-boats capable to blockading Britain into surrender. Germany's defeat in the First World War, the hated Versailles *Diktat* and fate of the German High Seas Fleet were humiliations Dönitz was determined to avenge. So it was that within days of the outbreak of the Second World War, Dönitz began planning what he would later describe in his memoirs as 'the boldest of bold enterprises': getting a U-boat into Scapa Flow, the most important British anchorage, to wreak havoc with the Royal Navy's Home Fleet.

Dönitz knew how safe the British felt at Scapa Flow, given the security precautions taken with anti-submarine nets, blockships, minefields, booms, guardships, patrols and searchlights. This could also be to his advantage, however, as such confidence bred complacency. But, with the loss of two German submarines which attempted to enter the Flow during the First World War still very much in mind, how could a U-boat penetrate those defences? Dönitz ordered his staff to collate every scrap of intelligence possible to facilitate the attack. By the end of that first month of war in 1939, the *Luftwaffe* provided detailed aerial photographs of Scapa Flow, from which Dönitz was able to study the defences. Seven entrances could be seen: an eastern approach through Holm Sound accessed three – Kirk, Skerry and East Weddel Sounds – and Water Sound was a separate 'gate'. Hoxa and Switha Sound lay to the south, but were both protected by booms, as was Hoy Sound to the north-west. From these photographs it was clear that a U-boat could only enter the Flow from the east, where there was a tight route between the blockships in Kirk Sound. Dönitz later wrote that:

> there is a narrow channel about 50 ft wide and 23 ft deep. To the north of the block ships is another, smaller, gap. The shore on both sides is practically uninhabited. I think that it would be possible to penetrate here – at night, on the surface and at slack water. The main difficulties will be navigational.

To strike a blow at the Royal Navy within that safest of bases, Dönitz knew, would be a great coup, shattering British morale. Weather experts advised that the best time for such an attack would, appropriately, be on the night of Friday, 13 October 1939, as both periods of slack water (when incoming and outgoing tides meet) occurred during a night lit by a full moon.

While U-boat Command planned their audacious sortie, on 17 September 1939 the Royal Navy suffered a demoralising loss: the aircraft carrier HMS *Courageous* was sunk by U-29; 518 British seamen were lost. The loss of this capital ship was, in fact, unnecessary and reflects the confusion regarding how best to combat the U-boat threat. Churchill, then First Sea Lord, required aggressive pro-activity against the German submarines, forming 'Hunter Killer Groups' to locate and destroy them using the new ASDIC radar and depth charges. Foolishly, however, these units included not only destroyers and other anti-submarine craft but also capital ships. The latter, of course, presented huge and slow targets, a fact taken full advantage of by U-29 that fateful day. As *Courageous* went down, it was perfectly clear that, as in the Great War, the U-boat was a menace to be reckoned with.

To carry out the attack on Scapa Flow, the obvious choice of weapon was a Type VIIB U-boat. The Type VII was the mainstay of the *U-Bootwaffe* throughout the war, and the 'B' variant the most advanced at that time. With a length of 66.5 metres, a bhp MAN diesel engine capable of 17.2 knots surfaced, while an electric motor provided 17.8 knots while submerged. Travelling on the surface at 12 knots, a Type VIIB's range was 6,500 nautical miles, and submerged at 4 knots could cover 90 nautical miles. Four torpedo tubes faced forward, one aft, and nine extra 'eels' (as torpedoes were nicknamed) were carried. An 8.8 cm gun was positioned on the deck forward of the conning tower, and a 2 cm cannon provided anti-aircraft defence. It took a crew of forty-four men to operate a Type VIIB, who lived in an almost intolerably cramped and damp environment. But which of his Type VIIBs and commanders would *Kommodore* Dönitz choose for this most dangerous of missions? There was one man cut from the same cloth as the *Kommodore* himself: *Kapitänleutnant* Günther Prien, commander of U-47.

The son of a judge, Prien was born in Osterfeld in January 1908, and by 1939, had spent half his thirty-one years at sea. In the early days he served on schooners and trade ships, joining the *Reichsmarine* in 1933. After a year aboard the light cruiser *Königsberg,* he transferred to U-boats and was commissioned. In 1938, Prien was on U-26, patrolling Spanish waters during the Civil War. When war was declared on 3 September 1939, *Kaleun* Prien was commanding U-47 and on patrol in the Bay of Biscay; there he soon chalked up three successes, all British merchant ships: *Bosnia, Rio Claro* and *Gartavon* all went to the bottom at the hands of U-47. Dönitz concluded that Prien 'possessed all the personal qualities and professional ability required'.

Prien's later memoir was essentially 'ghosted' by a propaganda writer and, as will be seen, is clearly and significantly at odds with the facts and evidence in certain regards. However, the description of how Prien came to be given the Scapa Flow mission can, I think, be considered accurate, and is worth quoting:

'After dinner we stood about chatting in the Mess of our depot ship. An orderly opened the door and *Kapitän* von Friedeburg entered. "Gentlemen, your attention please. *Korvettenkapitän* Sobe and *Kapitänleutnants* Wellmer and Prien are requested to report to the CO U-boats." He saluted and left.

'We looked at each other and my CO asked me, "What on earth is going on? What have you been up to? Have you been in a brawl or something?" He looked first at Wellmer and then at me. Wellmer answered for both of us: "No, sir." Ten minutes later we boarded a barge which was secured alongside and went over to the *Weichsel*. The harbour was peacefully quiet and we were silent too.

'I considered what the CO could want with us, for such a command is most unusual on a Sunday. My companions were also lost in thought.

'When we arrived on the *Weichsel* the crew of a U-boat paraded on the Tirpitz Mole; the *Kommodore* was inspecting them.

'We went into the Mess and waited. The minutes seemed like hours, until finally a runner came. Clicking his heels he said, "Will the *Kapitäns* please go to the CO of the U-boats in the Admiral's Mess."

'Sobe went first and was followed by Wellmer. I remained alone and slipping up to the window gazed outside. What on earth was coming now, I wondered? The thought was becoming unbearable.

'At last the runner returned. "Will *Kaleun* Prien please go to the CO." The runner preceded me up a few stairs and then I entered the large room. In the centre stood a large table covered in charts. Behind it stood the CO, Wellmer and Sobe.

"Beg to report present."

"Thank you, Prien". The CO shook my hand. "Now please listen carefully to Wellmer," he said, and, turning to Wellmer, "Wellmer, will you please begin from the beginning again."

Wellmer stepped up to the table and bent over the charts.

"The usual security measures are the same as always. The particular security measures which I reported in the war diary are at these points." He placed his finger several places on the charts.

'I followed him with my eyes. He was pointing at the Orkneys and in the centre of the charts was written in large letters *Bay of Scapa Flow*.

'Wellmer explained further, but at that moment I could hardly follow him, for my thoughts were milling around the name Scapa Flow. *Kommodore* Dönitz, the U-boat CO, who was in the group, said "During the Great War the British defence booms lay here." He leaned over the chart and indicated the places with the point of a compass. "In all probability they will be there again. In this place Emsmann was destroyed." The compass point rested on Hoxa Sound. "And here," a stroke with the compass, "are the usual anchorages of the British Fleet. All seven inlets to the bay will be boomed and well guarded. All the same, I think that a resolute commander could get through just here." The point of the compass wandered over the chart. "Mind you, it won't be an easy job because between the islands the current is very strong. All the same, I believe that it can be done."

'He raised his head and gazed at me searchingly under lowered brows. "What is your opinion, Prien?" I stared at the chart, but before I could answer the CO continued, "I don't want your answer now; think the matter over carefully, take all available information with you and study your chances. I shall expect your decision on Tuesday." I straightened up and he looked me in the eye: "I hope you have understood me, Prien. You are perfectly free to make your own decision. If you come to the conclusion that the undertaking is impossible, you will report that fact to me." He continued emphatically, "No blame whatsoever will be attached to you, Prien, because we know that your decision will be based on your own honest conviction." He shook me by the hand; I gathered up the charts and notes, saluted and left. I had myself taken out to the depot ship *Hamburg*. I locked the charts and notes away in a steel safe and then I went home.

'On the way soldiers and sailors saluted me but I returned their salutes mechanically. I felt a tremendous tension within me. Would it be possible to bring it off? My common sense calculated and questioned the chances, but my will had already decided that it could be brought off. At home, supper was already on the table. Absentmindedly I greeted my wife and child, for my thoughts were obsessed with the single idea of Scapa Flow. After supper I begged my wife to go out alone, for I still had work to do. "Oh yes, your next patrol." But she left without further comment or question, for she was a soldier's daughter.

'As soon as she had left, I returned to the depot ship *Hamburg*. I fetched the charts from the safe and took them home with me. Then I sat down at my desk and spread the charts and plans out before me. I worked through the whole thing like a mathematical problem. The care with which the defences had been planned was amazing. By the time I had finished it was already dark. Bunching the papers together I took them back to the *Hamburg*, through the dark and silent town. Only the stars glowed clear in the sky.

'Next morning I requested an interview with *Kapitän* von Friedeburg. He received me at once. "Well," he said, looking at me through narrowed eyes, "what do you think, Prien?"

"When may I report to the CO, sir?"

"So you are going?"

"Yes sir."

He dropped heavily into his chair and reached for the telephone. "I thought you Might," he said, "Only I wasn't sure on account of your wife and child." Then he spoke on the telephone, "Yes sir, Prien is with me now … very good sir … at 1400 hours, sir." He stood up.

"Two o'clock this afternoon you may see the CO," he said. "The big lion is waiting," he added.

'Punctually at two I was there. As I entered I found him at his desk. "Beg to report present, sir", I said. He did not acknowledge my salute; it seemed as if he hadn't noticed it. He was looking at me fixedly and asked, "Yes or no?"

"Yes sir."

The shadow of a smile flitted across his face. Then, seriously again, he asked "Have you thoroughly considered the whole business? Did you think of Emsmann and Henning?",

"Yes sir", I replied.

"Very well, get your boat ready", he said, "We will fix the departure time later on".

He got up, walked round the desk and shook my hand. He said nothing but his handshake was firm.

'We left on 8 October, at 10 o'clock in the morning. It was again a beautiful clear Sunday. *Kapitän* von Friedeburg stood on the pier with the adjutant of the Chief of the Flotilla. For a short while I stood with them on the wall, looking over to the little boat was made fast to the stakes. The crew were already on board.

'We were walking up and down the pier, hardly saying a word. Only right at the end von Friedeburg said, "Well, Prien, whatever happens you are sure of many thousands of tons, and now, best of luck my boy." I saluted and walked across the gangway to the boat.

'The ropes were cast off and the roar of the diesels thundered through the boat. Then we were slowly making our way for the green sea, our course nor'nor'west and our objective Scapa Flow.'

And so it was that in the autumn of 1939, sudden and violent death stalked beneath the North Sea, towards the peaceful Orkneys.

Confident that Scapa Flow was safe from submarine or surface attack, the Home Fleet's main fear was being struck from the air. German reconnaissance bombers operating from Norway were regularly over the Orkneys, photographing and studying the anchorage, but, as we have seen, this was not necessarily with an air attack in mind. All of this invaluable information was being fed to *Kommodore* Dönitz, who was planning the impossible: to penetrate the Orkney defences with a U-boat which, once within the Flow, would wreak havoc upon the Home Fleet.

On 26 September 1939, the Home Fleet, including such capital ships as *Nelson, Rodney, Hood, Renown* and *Ark Royal,* left the Orkneys and forayed across the North Sea; during the return trip, Ju 88 dive-bombers of KG 30, operating from Westerland/Sylt, pounced. *Leutnant* Storp achieved a direct hit on HMS *Hood,* but his bomb bounced off the ship into the sea without causing any damage. *Gefreiter* Francke recorded a near miss alongside the aircraft carrier HMS *Ark Royal,* although the German propaganda machine soon whirred into action and announced that the great ship had been sunk. Having the whole Home Fleet concentrated together at anchor in Scapa Flow, however, clearly made easy targets for the *Luftwaffe,* a fact the Commander-in-Chief, Admiral Sir Charles Forbes, was acutely aware of.

On 8 October 1939, the German Fleet Commander, Admiral Hermann Bohm, made a clever sortie up the Norwegian coast towards the Utsire Light with his flagship, the *Gneisenau,* the cruiser *Koln,* and nine destroyers. Bohm's intention was two-fold: first, to provide a diversion for the pocket battleships *Graf Spee* and *Deutschland,* heading for the South Atlantic, and second, to entice the Home Fleet out of Scapa Flow to be attacked by a large force of *Luftwaffe* bombers. The enemy ships were spotted by an RAF Lockheed Hudson reconnaissance aircraft, and the Admiralty decided that the *Gneisenau* was attempting to break out into the Atlantic and must therefore be stopped. Admiral Forbes was ordered to give chase and engage, his Humber Force subsequently sailing from Rosyth, and the Home Fleet from Scapa Flow. Ironically, this diversionary enterprise by Bohm, who was unaware that U-47 was leaving Kiel that day, bound for Scapa Flow on the 'boldest of bold enterprises', would ultimately rob Prien of the rich pickings he expected to find.

The *Gneisenau* diversion was actually unsuccessful for all involved, on both sides. RAF Wellington bombers were dispatched to attack the enemy fleet, but failed to find it, and likewise the *Luftwaffe* missed the Home Fleet (in spite of flying 148 sorties). The Germans did bomb the lesser Humber Force, but without success, and the four U-boats briefed to take part made no contact whatsoever. Bohm managed to pass safely undetected through the Kattegat back to Kiel, and on 9 October, Forbes ordered both his Humber Force and Home Fleet back to Scotland. During Forbes' foray across the North Sea, the weather was awful, and *Royal Oak* had been unable to keep up with the Home Fleet, so it seemed thereafter that the ship's future lay in static harbour AA defence, or perhaps bombardment, or as a 'long stop' in the complex manoeuvres required to head off German warships. Fatefully, *Royal Oak*, therefore, returned to Scapa Flow.

With the spectre of air attack at the forefront of his mind, Admiral Forbes returned Humber Force to the Forth, but decided against returning the Home Fleet to Scapa Flow. Instead, and most wisely as indicated by subsequent events, Forbes dispersed his ships: HMS *Hood,* HMS *Nelson* and HMS *Rodney* were sent to Loch Ewe on the west coast, while HMS *Sheffield* stayed at sea. Only HMS *Royal Oak* (a battleship), HMS *Repulse* (a battle cruiser), HMS *Furious* (an old aircraft carrier), HMS *Newcastle* and HMS *Aurora* (both cruisers) returned to Scapa Flow. First to arrive was HMS *Royal Oak,* at 0705 hrs on 11 October 1939, the venerable old warrior taking station in the north-east corner of the anchorage, her guns therefore able to offer antiaircraft protection to both Kirkwall and the radar station at nearby Netherburton. The following afternoon, a *Luftwaffe* reconnaissance flight identified a total of sixty-three naval ships at Scapa Flow, this information being fed to Dönitz who therefore fully expected U-47, scheduled to attack the next night, to find many targets. After that German aircraft passed overhead and took those final photographs before Prien's attack, however, nine vessels sailed from Scapa Flow, the most important of which being HMS *Repulse,* which went to Rosyth. Throughout the day on Friday, 13 October 1939, and as usual, Scapa Flow saw ships come and go. At 1520 hrs, the Royal Navy's latest and largest cruiser, HMS *Belfast,* anchored off Flotta, in the main area of the Flow. HMS *Royal Oak,* however, remained in the north-east corner, together with the twenty-five-year old aircraft carrier HMS *Pegasus,* and just 1,000 yards offshore.

Bert Pocock remembers:

> I joined the *Royal Oak* at Portsmouth in June 1939. We sailed to Weymouth where I was a member of the party detailed to collect the Royal Family's baggage from the local station and convey it to the Royal Yacht. *Royal Oak* then sailed to Scapa Flow. I was a Boy 1st Class, and I thought it was great to be in the Royal Navy; little did I know what dark days there were ahead.
>
> At Scapa Flow we anchored in Kirkwall Bay, and were there when war was declared on Germany, September 3rd, 1939. A big cheer went up from the crew, boy, were we going to show 'em! The officers were called together by the Captain, W.H. Benn, and drank the toast 'Damnation to the enemy'. Then the First Lord of the Admiralty, Winston Churchill himself, came aboard and spoke to us. It was inspiring.
>
> Then we were sent out on patrol. The sea was really rough, there was six in of water splashing around the Boys' Mess Deck, as a result of which it was only possible to sleep on the tables and benches there. So, it was good to get back into Kirkwall Bay and have a run ashore for a couple of days.

Another Boy 1st Class, of which there were many aboard *Royal Oak*, was Arthur Smith:

> I was just 16 years old when, on 1 June 1938, I walked through the gates of HMS *St Vincent,* a boys' training establishment, to begin ten months of hard work, hard, but fair, discipline, and a

thorough grounding in the workings of the senior service. March 1939, saw me, together with my classmates, joining HMS *Hawkins,* a cruiser of the Reserve Fleet tied up in Portsmouth Harbour and one of only two ships in the Royal Navy armed with 7.5-inch guns (the other being HMS *Frobisher).* There we became conversant with every aspect of shipboard life, with the exception of watch-keeping (a pleasure yet to come!). I enjoyed my time aboard this ship as there was a slight lessening of the rigid discipline, and the opportunity to have a (duty free) cigarette without the fear of eighteen cuts across the backside with a cane was bliss. I really began to feel like a sailor. However, all good things come to an end, and in June of 1939, together with 200 other Boys, I was drafted to HMS *Royal Oak,* to form part of the ship's company. This was again in Portsmouth.

I was now 17 and about to experience five and a half months of misery. I am afraid to say that *Royal Oak* was not a happy ship, especially, for Boy Seamen. Some ships are happy, others not; it was hard to put your finger on why she was an unhappy ship, but unhappy she certainly was. Luckily it was my only experience of this kind. Anyone who has not experienced the difference between a happy and unhappy ship cannot begin to imagine the effect that this atmosphere can have on shipboard life.

When war was declared, my Action Station was in the 'A' Turret Shell-Room, which meant that I only did four-hour watches at sea and enjoyed all night in my hammock while in harbour. However, on Sunday October 8th, on my way to the NAAFI to buy a bar of chocolate, I was passing the Gunnery Office when I was called by the Chief Gunner's Mate, who demanded to know where my Action Station was. When I told him 'A' Shell-Room, he replied 'Not any more, it is now S1 four-inch AA gun. One of the gun's crew is in Sick Bay with appendicitis, and you are his replacement.' I cursed my luck at this, as AA crews kept watch in harbour, which obviously meant losing my all-night in.

> At that time I was unaware that this unexpected turn of events while going to get a bar of chocolate would be instrumental in saving my life a few days later.

Ken Toop was also a Boy 1st Class, who had likewise been through training at HMS *St Vincent* and HMS *Hawkins*:

> When one joins a ship, the choice of hammock slinging hooks are limited because the first ones to join sling wherever they choose. Boys, for obvious reasons, are required to sling in the Boys' Mess Deck, under the watchful eye of the Boys' Instructor and PTI. But because there were more bodies than hooks, on HMS *Royal Oak* I had to find a hook elsewhere, which was in the Port Six Inch Gun No 2 working space. In the next hammock to mine was a Boy called McCarthy.

Again, Ken's forced alternative sleeping arrangements would soon play an unexpected part in saving his life.

On the night of Friday, 13 October 1939, the crew of HMS *Royal Oak* settled into their bunks and hammocks, having re-provisioned and cleaned up the mess caused by heavy seas during the *Gneisenau* patrol. Safe at anchor within impregnable Scapa Flow, the ship's company, excepting the few on watch, gratefully settled down to sleep.

When U-47 left Kiel, only the *Kaleun,* Günther Prien, knew that the boat's destination was Scapa Flow. His crew were puzzled as the smoke trails of ships beyond the horizon were not investigated, as the boat ploughed on nor'nor'west. Gradually the weather worsened, the barometer fell and a gale began – the same storm that was simultaneously making life uncomfortable for HMS *Royal Oak* on the *Gneisenau* patrol. U-boats were designed to travel mostly on the surface, using their powerful diesel engines, submerging only to avoid detection and sometimes attack (so in reality these were more accurately 'diving boats' rather than submarines). As U-47 fought the gale, those on watch swathed in oilskins but still drenched by the cold North Sea, eventually, through the darkness, saw the shadow of land. Prien's second-in-command, *Oberleutnant* Englebert Endrass asked his captain if they were to 'visit the Orkneys?' Prien's response being, 'We are going to Scapa Flow,' which would have shaken a lesser man. Endrass simply replied 'That will be OK Sir, that will be quite OK.'

On 12 October 1939, U-47 lay submerged during the day, just off the Orkneys, surfacing during the evening and approaching the coast to fix the boat's exact position. At 0437 hrs on Friday, 13 October, U-47 gently settled on the seabed, 90 metres below the surface, just off the Orkneys. It was then that Prien decided to tell his crew of their mission. Assembling the men in the Forrard Mess, the news was greeted with absolute silence. Prien (as he later wrote in his memoir) issued instructions:

> Everyone except the watch will go to their bunks and sleep, the watch will wake the cook at 1400 hrs. At 1600 hrs we will have dinner. Then for the duration of the mission there will be no more hot food. Only cold sandwiches at all stations. And everyone will have a slab of chocolate. All superfluous light will be extinguished, we must economise on electricity; no one is to move unnecessarily, for we shall be lying aground for this evening and must be careful with the air. During the mission there is to be absolute silence. No message is to be repeated.

Dismissed, the crew of U-47 went to their bunks. Prien tried but was unable to sleep. In the Ward Room he found his navigator, Spahr, pouring over his charts, before returning to his bunk and sleeping until 1400 hrs, when the Watch went to wake the cook, creeping past the *Kaleun*'s bunk with his feet wrapped in cloth so as to ensure perfect silence. At 1600 hrs, as per Prien's orders, the crew was wakened and enjoyed a substantial hot meal of veal cutlets and green cabbage. Tables were then cleared and charges fixed with which to scuttle the boat should the mission fail and U-47 fall into enemy hands. Prien reiterated his instructions: during the entire action smoking and unnecessary talking were forbidden. Lifejackets were checked. Two 'eels' were placed in the rapid loading position before tubes one and two. In the boat's log, Prien noted that the crew's morale was 'splendid'.

At 1900 hrs, U-47 surfaced to periscope depth. Prien scanned the area, confirming it was safe. At 1915 hrs, the grey submarine slid from beneath the waves and surfaced. The conning tower hatch was opened, allowing fresh air to rush in, and Prien, two officers and his Bo'sun quickly scrambled up onto the open bridge, clad in cumbersome oilskins. The wind had dropped; the swell was much reduced, and all around was clear of the enemy. Fans were started to ventilate the boat, electric motors stopped and diesel engines started. Prien set course for Holm Sound: there was no turning back now.

At 2307 hrs, just before Rose Ness, U-47 sighted an unidentified merchant ship and dived, remaining submerged until 2331 hrs when the boat surfaced in Holm Sound, the entrance to Kirk and Skerry Sounds. So close to land, U-47's diesel engines were too noisy, so Prien switched over to the much stealthier electric motors. Cloud cover was light, the night bright and clear, and across the entire horizon danced the Northern Lights, something that the planners had not anticipated. In Skerry Sound, Prien could clearly see the blockship there and as a result, wrongly believed he was in Kirk Sound. Spahr, using dead reckoning, contested the boat's presumed position, and Prien soon realised his mistake. Altering course hard to starboard, collision was avoided, and just a few minutes later Kirk Sound was clearly visible.

In his boat's log, Prien wrote:

> It is a very eerie sight. On land everything is dark, high in the sky are the flickering Northern Lights, so that the Bay, surrounded by highish mountains, is directly lit from above. The blockships lie in the Sound, as ghostly as the wings of a theatre.

Prien's conscientious and thorough study of his charts now paid off. Deciding to pass through on the northern side of the blockships, following a course of 270, U-47 passed the first one with 315 metres to spare. Then a strong current hit the boat from starboard, simultaneously Prien spotted the cable of the northernmost blockship, the *Soriano,* lying at an angle of 45° ahead. With port engine stopped, starboard engine slow ahead, and rudder hard to port, the tricky current was negotiated, although the U-boat scraped along the bottom and its stern caught the cable. Slowly the boat eased free, and, turning to port and with some 'difficult rapid manoeuvring', resumed course. A combination of tide and electric motor power then swept U-47 into St Mary's Bay; Prien had achieved the impossible: U-47 was now safely within Scapa Flow and still undetected. Quite simply, the *Kaleun* announced 'We are inside.' At that point, however, the whole mission was nearly scuppered; as the boat passed the village of St Mary's, just half a mile away, the headlights of a car suddenly illuminated U-47. Fortunately for Prien, no alarm was raised and the car turned and continued towards Kirkwall.

In U-47's all-important log, Prien recorded that at 0027 hrs on Saturday, 14 October 1939:

> It is disgustingly light. The whole Bay is lit up. To the south of Cava there is nothing. I go farther in. To port, I recognise the Hoxa Sound coastguard, to which, in the next few minutes, the boat must present itself as a target. In that event, all would be lost; at present south of Cava no ships are to be seen, although visibility is extremely good.

Finding no targets to the south, Prien turned U-47 north, creeping along the coast. The log records that at 0055 hrs, 'Two battleships are lying there at anchor, and, further inshore, destroyers. Cruisers not visible, therefore attack on the big fellows. Distance apart 3,000 metres.' Prien had found the old battleship HMS *Royal Oak,* bows to the north-east, and the ancient aircraft carrier HMS *Pegasus,* slumbering peacefully in the north-east corner of Scapa Flow and in the lee of Kirkwall's cliffs. The excitement felt by Prien and those with him on U-47's bridge can only be imagined; later, Prien wrote:

> At last, over there … close to the shore appeared the mighty silhouette of a battleship. Hard and clear, as if painted into the sky with black ink. The bridge, the mighty funnel and aft, like filigree, the tall mast. Slowly we edged closer. At such a moment all feeling stopped. One became part of the boat, the brain of this

steel animal which was creeping up towards its enormous prey.

At such a time you must think in iron and steel-or perish.

In the heat of the moment, however, the old aircraft carrier *Pegasus* was identified as HMS *Repulse,* a most desirable target, although because of its position, *Royal Oak* would have to be attacked first. The 'eels' were made ready.

As U-47 turned to starboard, at around 0100 hrs, Endrass gave the order for all four forward torpedo tubes to fire. One 'eel' jammed, the other three sped towards their target. Spahr counted down the seconds to impact: 5, 10, 15, 20. Turning around, Prien fired his stern tube. Some four minutes later a single explosion was heard (it being suspected that the *Repulse* had been hit), but to those watching from the bridge of U-47, *Royal Oak* appeared unaffected. Still on the surface and aware that detection was doubtless imminent, Prien fired another three torpedoes from the bow. Prien describes the consequent destruction:

> Now something occurred that no one had anticipated and no one who had seen it would ever forget. A wall of water shot up towards the sky. It was as if the sea suddenly stood up on end. Loud explosions came one after the other like drumfire in a battle and coalesced into one mighty ear-splitting crash. Flames shot skyward, blue … yellow … red.
>
> Behind this hellish firework display the sky disappeared completely. Like huge birds, black shadows soared through the flames, fell hissing and splashing into the water. Fountains yards high sprang up where they had fallen, huge fragments of the mast and funnels. We must have hit the ammunition magazine and the deadly cargo had torn the body of its own ship apart.
>
> I could not take my eyes from the glass. It was as if the gates of hell had suddenly been torn open and I was looking into the flaming furnace. I glanced down into my boat. Down there it was dark and still. I could hear the hum of the motors. Spahr's even voice and the answers of the planesman. I felt as never before

my kinship with these men below who did their duty silently and blindly, who could neither see the day nor the target, and died in the dark if it had to be. I called down 'He's finished!' For a moment there was silence. Then a mighty roar went through the boat, an almost bestial roar in which the pent-up tension of the past twenty-four hours found release.

At 0014 hrs, Prien's first torpedo had hit the starboard bow of HMS *Royal Oak*, one plate below the waterline, the resulting explosion tearing a hole 40–50 ft wide and three plates deep. Captain Benn was advised that the most likely explanation was merely an internal explosion in the ship's inflammable store. That a torpedo was responsible was not even a consideration. Arthur Smith, however, remembers:

> At midnight I took up position on SI four inch on the Four Inch Gun Deck for the middle watch, 0000–0400 hrs, to be told that I was to make my way up to the starboard wing of the bridge, where I would perform the duty of aircraft lookout. The night being as black as it was, I didn't fancy my chances of seeing any if they did fly over, but orders are orders so up I went. I remember thinking how cold it was, when the ship literally jumped to a massive explosion, directly below me on the starboard side. A column of water shot up, while the port anchor chain ran out, the cable roaring across the fo'csle unchecked and making an incredible noise. It didn't take a genius to work out that we had been torpedoed, but how could that be? We were in Scapa Flow, a secure anchorage; little did we know how insecure it really was until much later. Action Stations was piped, so I ran down to the Four Inch Gun Deck to join my gun's crew. There was considerable speculation as to the cause of the explosion, and when I said that we'd been torpedoed I got a clip around the ear from the captain of the gun crew and told not to be such an idiot, and only speak when spoken to! Talk about boys should be seen but not heard! After about fifteen minutes, Fall Out from

Action Stations was piped, the majority of the ship's company hopping back into their hammocks while I was sent back up to my lookout position.

Bert Pocock:

Just after midnight there was an almighty bang, which I felt good and proper as my hammock was up against the side of a ladder. Being on the short side this meant I was able to climb up the ladder and step into my hammock, instead of having to swing in. It was this that saved my life. With that bang, all we Boys jumped out of our hammocks, wondering what had happened. A Chief Petty Officer came running through on his way forward and told us to get back in our hammocks, so back in our hammocks we went. At least fifty hammocks were slung in the Boys' After Mess Deck, very crowded by today's standards. I looked across to my three fellow Reading townies and gave a smile with thumbs up. Then things quietened down a bit.

Alf Fordham was a Musician in the Royal Marines, having joined as a 'Band Boy' in 1933 when just 14½. He had served on HMS *Royal Oak* since 1937:

I was asleep in my hammock when I and many others, were woken by a noise, and the ship shuddered. Nobody knew what had occurred; no one would have thought it was a torpedo in harbour. I stayed in my hammock, which probably saved my life. I saw the Gunnery Officer pass by, looking very worried. Then through the Tannoy 'Take magazine temperatures', which sounded very worrying.

Ken Toop:

After 'Pipe Down', the ship's passages below deck are lit by lights low down on the bulkhead. When the first torpedo struck, forward on the starboard side, I was asleep and did not hear it. McCarthy got up and went to investigate, returning saying 'You'd better get out, Lofty, something's happened.' So I hurriedly got my trousers and shoes on, which was, fortunately as it turned out, protection for my back and feet. I attempted to climb the Midship Companion Way, as the emergency lights were still on, but there were a lot of chaps all with the same idea, so I made my way forward through the screen door.

While a certain amount of concern and confusion swept through the ship, many sailors, below decks and in their hammocks, went back to sleep, dismissing the interruption as an internal problem and not particularly serious. Others, like Toop and McCarthy, felt uneasy and made their way on deck.

Those watching from the bridge of U-47 were confused as to why the two other forward-firing torpedoes, and the one from astern, had not exploded. Unbeknown to them, their electrical torpedoes at that early stage of the war were unreliable, sometimes running too deep, or erratically, on occasion exploding too soon, sometimes too late. Having reloaded the three operational bow tubes, Prien fired a salvo of three more 'eels' at *Royal Oak*. This time, the effect was catastrophic.

Arthur Smith:

> Hardly had I resumed my position as aircraft lookout that the ship rocked to three more explosions, again from the starboard side. Almost immediately the ship listed to starboard and I was pretty sure that she was finished. When the order to 'Abandon Ship' was piped I immediately ran down to the Four Inch Gun Deck, which I intended to jump off, and one of my most vivid memories of that night was struggling to release the toggles of my duffel coat with cold fingers. By the time this was accomplished there was no time left to divest myself of boots and uniform, so into the sea I went, fully clothed.

FACES OF HMS ROYAL OAK

Alf Fordham:

> About ten minutes after being awakened came the most violent explosion which seemed to lift the ship out of the water. We all jumped out of our hammocks.

Bert Pocock:

> About ten minutes after the first bang there was another, bigger bang that nearly threw me out of my hammock. Out went the lights, and you could feel the ship starting to list starboard. Chief or no Chief I knew there was trouble, so with the ladder alongside of me it was up and through the escape/hatch (as the big main hatch was down because the ship was only on standby), which only one man could pass through at a time. As I went through the hatch I lined myself up for the next ladder heading up to the Galley Deck. I then started to move forward with my arms out and moving my legs around to feel anything, as it seemed darker than dark. I said to myself 'Mum, help me out of this one!' It seemed like a lifetime but I caught hold of the ladder and you could still feel the deck going over. As I was going up the ladder I called out 'Anybody there?' but the only sound to be heard was a loud hissing. I was hopeful that there was an answer, as I was scared going up alone in the darkness. I knew that the next ladder was only a yard away on the Galley Deck, and that this led out into the night, which was fairly dark. I had to go on all fours to the ship's side, working towards the bows, going slowly into the sea, as they say you can get sucked back into the ship when going down. Once in the sea I swam like mad away from the ship.

Ken Toop:

> The ship was starting to list to starboard, so much so that I was able to leave over the port side, sliding down and stepping on

the slight ledge where the anti-torpedo blisters joined the ship's side. By clambering and crawling I managed to make my way aft along the side towards the stern, where the drifter *Daisy*, attached to the ship as a tender while in harbour, was tied up alongside – but by this time the ship was turning over onto its starboard side and so the *Daisy* had to be cast off, or she would have floundered. I was left with no option but to move up the side towards the keel, until sliding into the sea was unavoidable. I entered into a thick covering of oil fuel on a freezing sea.

Pocock and Toop were lucky to escape. The first torpedo of this second salvo hit *Royal Oak* roughly amidships and below the Boys' Mess Deck, killing and maiming many of the young sailors in their hammocks there. Indeed, it was this explosion that had nearly thrown Pocock from his hammock. Following that explosion the ship came alive, men all over jumping from their hammocks, but then there was another hit, this time further aft on the starboard side; a hole was torn in the armoured deck and killed many men in the Stokers' Mess Deck. When the electricity supply subsequently failed, the ship was plunged into darkness, accentuating the panic and chaos below decks. Without power, it was impossible for orders to be transmitted over the Tannoy, or send a distress signal. As *Royal Oak* listed, water poured in through portholes, the glass having been removed and replaced with ventilators while the crew was at anchor. The seawater rushing into the ship increased the chaos and suffering within, and hastened the ship's instability.

Then the 'hellish firework display' described by Prien started. Alf Fordham:

> I stopped to put my trousers on, that delay saving my life: had I run forward immediately, in an effort to gain the Quarter Deck, I would have run into the most intensely hot orange flame, which shot through the door; because I had stood still it missed me by a few feet. A cordite magazine had exploded and vented wherever it could.

Had Fordham run into that white hot flame, it would have cremated him on the spot, sadly the fate of many sailors. Everything flammable touched by that blowtorch went up in flames. He continues:

> Seeing this I reversed my direction. Because the lights were out it was pitch dark. A group of us tried to open the door leading aft through the officers' quarters, but I couldn't get the cleats off properly in the dark. After a minute or two, Musician 'Ned' Kelly – bless him – shouted 'Stand back, stand back' and methodically went around the many cleats and successfully got the door open, through which many men poured.
>
> I reached the Quarter Deck and dimly through the darkness saw dozens of men attempting to get on *Daisy,* the drifter tied alongside. After a few minutes I suddenly realised that the deck was listing beneath my feet, so I ran to the stern, intending to jump off, but didn't make it. Suddenly I slipped down some distance and hit the water, going down miles it seemed. As I surfaced, something touched my back and I thought the ship was coming down on top of me, so I did a very fast swim away. It was so dark that I had not seen the ship going over to starboard, nor seen her sink. The water was extremely cold and I was covered in thick oil.

On the tender *Daisy II,* a quick thinking crewman, Johnnie Duthie, saved her from going under by cutting the rope holding her to the doomed battleship, which sank below Scapa Flow in less than ten minutes. With the sea around him covered in thick black oil and screaming men, the tender's skipper, John Gatt, suddenly found himself directing a major rescue operation.

Able Seaman Stanley Cole was among those men in the water:

> I could smell the oil-fuel, but could not avoid getting some in the mouth, nose and ears; I kept my eyes closed until I surfaced. Coughing and spluttering, I became aware that my right foot and leg seemed to be hanging in the water as I began to swim away from the ship's side, along with some others. It was like trying

to swim through liquid tar, and I was convinced that I wasn't going to make it.

The water was bitterly cold, and from all around me in the darkness I could hear cries for help from injured, burned and despairing bodies. Kicking out as best I could with my good leg, I was sure that I could feel the bodies of drowned shipmates under my foot. Then my hand caught something, a piece of wood about 2 ft long by 6 in wide, so I hung on to it in the blind faith that it would keep me afloat – I would have killed anyone who tried to take it from me! Then another stroke of luck: what I took to be a five gallon oil drum came within range and I tried to hold my arm over it, as it slipped and rolled with the oil. Finally, after what seemed like ages, I made out three or four bobbing heads paddling slowly along a length of timber, which I suppose could have been one of the 'deals' we adapted for seating at church services etc. I let go of the drum but not my small scrap of wood, and joined up with the lads paddling the deal. We tried shouting and singing, our throats hoarse, but without success, growing colder and more exhausted. One of our number slipped off the plank and we never saw him again.

My last view of *Royal Oak* was of her keel, silhouetted against the dark skyline. She appeared to have turned right over. Then, just as I had all but given up the struggle, along came a ship's whaler and I felt myself hauled over the boat's side, with two or three other lads dumped on top of me in a cold, sodden, oily heap.

While the individual bodies were being taken from the water, the crew of the drifter *Daisy II,* under the command of skipper John Gatt, were valiantly picking men up until *Daisy* herself was in danger of capsizing under the sheer weight of numbers.

Ken Toop:

Once in the sea I managed to take off my shoes and trousers, which had saved me from barnacle cuts off the ship's bottom, which I had slid down into the water. I was not a strong swimmer, having only met the Royal Navy's minimum standard (three lengths of the open air baths at HMS *St Vincent* and staying afloat for three minutes in a canvas duck suit). Nothing, though, prepares one for oil-fuel covered winter coldness of Scapa Flow, but eventually I managed to bump into a catamaran, a hefty wooden frame which was hoisted over the side by the crane when the ship was riding alongside a jetty, so I managed to climb onto it; two other half-dead men were already on it.

We floated around for I don't know how long, and the *Daisy* eventually picked us up. There were oil covered bodies everywhere. Some had to be put down into the fish hold, others lying round the funnel. The skipper made his way over to HMS *Pegasus,* where we spent the night trying to clean the fuel off us, which was impossible with only hard soap: no shampoo or detergents back then.

Bert Pocock:

I started to swim for the shore, as I felt more at ease out in the open, and I was a very good swimmer. Then I saw the trawler *Daisy* and went after it. By the time I was pulled aboard they said that *Royal Oak* had gone under. I shed a few tears, knowing that my fellow Reading townies had no chance of getting out.

Gatt's crew of six, Orkney fishermen all, rescued 360 men from those freezing oily waters, but were grief stricken as they had to pull away and heard the cries of 'Don't leave us *Daisy*' from doomed sailors left in the water.

Arthur Smith:

When I went into the sea, the ship's launch, a large boat, was still tied up to the starboard boom, so I climbed aboard with quite a few others. By this time, though, *Royal Oak* had listed at an angle preventing us from releasing the launch from the boom, as the painter was like an iron ball. I came to the conclusion that things were becoming rather dangerous, so, once again, I took to the sea. By this time the ship was going over rapidly, and I decided that the sooner I departed the scene the safer I would be. I hadn't gone far when she turned turtle, displacing a large wave which grabbed me, turning me over and over and down. I was totally helpless, but thankfully didn't panic, and kept kicking out in the hope of reaching the surface, which eventually I did, but not before taking in a couple of breaths of water which was most unpleasant. How I blessed my old dad at that moment for chucking me in the deep end of the local swimming baths when I was 5 years old and teaching me to swim.

Suddenly all the yelling, screaming and explosions stopped, and a deathly silence reigned. I knew that she had gone. I did not know, of course, how many hundreds of my shipmates had gone with her, which in retrospect was probably a good thing. I tried floating on my back for a while, until I heard voices not too far off. Swimming over to investigate I found a Carley life raft which was rather overloaded, so, with what I suppose was the optimism of youth, I decided to go solo; another reason was my dislike of the officer sitting on the raft issuing orders!

Remembering that when I went on watch, shore side was to starboard, and having jumped over on the starboard side, I struck out in the direction I was facing, believing that I would eventually hit land. Wrong! Striking out strongly with what we used to call the side stroke, I headed for the middle of Scapa Flow – away from shore! Ignorant of this fact, I felt faintly confident that in time I would set foot on dry land, as I was young and strong and supremely fit having boxed and played football to a high standard. As I was swimming alone I heard splashing and came upon another lad whose navigation had proved as bad as mine. Having established identities (he was also ex-*St Vincent* and *Hawkins*) we concentrated on our swimming in silence, when he suddenly said 'Oh bollocks to this' and disappeared under the water. I think that scared me more than anything that had gone on before, to think that a young 17-year-old could give up the ghost with no fuss or commotion. Poor lad had just reached the end of his tether.

Time stood still for me then and I was very cold, my boots weighed a ton and proved impossible to remove, due to the slimy coating of fuel-oil. The clothing was no problem, and maybe helped keep some warmth in my body. Although still swimming my strength was rapidly deserting me. I probably started to hallucinate, seeing my mother and knowing how she would react if I was to die. This probably gave me the incentive to carry on to the bitter end. Even so, I'd just about had it when I heard a voice say 'Here's another one', and I was grabbed and hauled into a boat, manned, by all people, four men of the RAF! It transpired that they were crewmen from the *Pegasus,* an old Great War catapult ship. When they heard the explosions they launched a boat and investigated. They saved three or four of us and I am truly glad that I had the strength left to thank them when they put us aboard their ship, where I was taken to a boiler room, my uniform and boots cut off and, standing in that lovely warm place, washed down with paraffin and cotton waste, given a blanket and a tot of rum which, combined with my exertions, knocked me right out.

According to Prien's memoir – which becomes unreliable at this point, written as it was to be a morale boosting piece of propaganda – after the final three explosions the anchorage then sprang into action, U-47 immediately changing from hunter to hunted. This was actually far from the truth, as there was no reaction from the defenders. Survivor Arthur Smith comments:

> Over the years since I have read many books and articles by people who claim to have been at Scapa Flow on the night of October 13/14th, 1939, in which they describe destroyers dashing about dropping depth-charges, guns being fired, and searchlights illuminating the scene. Prien said that the Northern Lights were evident; well, I saw and heard none of it, and I am neither deaf nor blind.

In his log, Prien justified his decision to withdraw at that point given that his periscope did not permit him to conduct submerged attacks at night, he could not be expected to manoeuvre unseen any longer on the surface and in any case he was sure that the driver of the car at St Mary's had seen, and therefore gone to report, U-47; moreover, he believed that further north within the anchorage lay unseen destroyers.

With both engines running at high speed, U-47 withdrew. At Skildaenoy Point, low tide and current worked against Prien, as again indicated by the boat's log:

> I must leave by the south, through the narrows, because of the depth of water. Things are again difficult. Course 058, slow – 10 knots. I make no progress. At high I pass the southern blockship with nothing to spare. The helmsman does magnificently. High speed ahead both … Free of the blockships – ahead a mole! Hard over and again about, and at 0215 hrs we are once more outside. A pity that only one was destroyed. The torpedo misses, I explain, are due to faults of course, speed and drift. In tube 4, a misfire. The crew behaved splendidly throughout the operation.

To his crew, Prien announced: 'All stations. Attention. One battleship destroyed, one battleship damaged – and we are through!'

FACES OF HMS ROYAL OAK

The relief among U-47's crew must have been unimaginable. With five torpedoes left, Prien set course for base.

Behind him, Prien had left death, destruction and misery. HMS *Royal Oak* lay 32 metres beneath Scapa Flow, and 835 of her crew were lost with her. The survivors were grateful to be alive, but in shock.

Ken Toop:

> Having spent what was left of that fateful night aboard *Pegasus,* the next day we were taken over to the battleship HMS *Iron Duke,* lying off Lyness, to have reports taken from us regarding our position on the *Royal Oak* and how we escaped. The next day we were taken by ferry to Scrabster, on the mainland, and by bus to Thurso. There we were put into civilian houses for a couple of days until we travelled by train to Portsmouth in our survivors' outfits. It took weeks to get the oil-fuel out of our hair and off our bodies, especially those that had the misfortune to swallow some. We were then sent on survivors' leave within a day or so, no way of letting our poor parents know any details, just a brief letter from Thurso confirming that we were alive and an announcement in the *Sunday Graphic* with a list of survivors, and that was it, we arrived home with a few shillings pay. Boys' pay was eight shillings and ninepence a week, but we all came from poor families; I had two small sisters and a father who was 60. He had lost an eye when only 7, but still served in the army during the Great War. So, at the end of ten days survivors' leave it was back to the dockyard at Portsmouth to join the cruiser HMS *Manchester* – shortly to leave for Scapa to spend the winter in Icelandic waters and on Northern Patrol until the Norwegian campaign started.
>
> According to my records, the number of Boy Seamen, Boy Telegraphists and Boy Signalmen aboard HMS *Royal Oak* was 163. Only thirty-seven were saved. In spite of reports to the

contrary, I still say that the ship sank in just a little over seven minutes.

Having also been rescued by *Daisy II,* Alf Fordham recalls the aftermath:

Aboard HMS *Pegasus* we were given, with much kindness, rum, cocoa, a bath and clean clothes. The next morning we were taken to the SS *Voltaire* to await transport south. Then another unexpected experience. We were lying off Lyness and experienced our first air raid. The old battleship *Iron Duke,* being used as a depot ship, was damaged. We were very nervous on the *Voltaire,* a huge liner – it seemed such a good target.

Later we were taken by train to Thurso and joined our train to go south. During the night's journey we were awakened by a bang and the carriage shook violently. A goods train was being shunted onto the same line – fortunately we were both moving slowly so no one was hurt.

What was left of our Royal Marines band, ten survivors out of fifteen musicians, arrived at Deal. We were kitted out with new uniforms and sent on survivors' leave.

Bert Pocock:

The night before we left by train for Portsmouth, we were put up by residents in Kirkwall. They were extremely kind to us, a lovely lot of people. I subsequently served on HMS *Manchester,* on which I could not have had a worse action station: the Telephone Exchange, right down in the bottom of the ship with hatch slammed down and clamped from outside. When we went into action we prayed that we did not get hit because we could not get out. Of the thirty-seven Boys who survived the *Royal Oak,* only eighteen, including myself, saw the war through.

FACES OF HMS ROYAL OAK

Arthur Smith:

> The following day we boarded the *Voltaire,* which was brought to life and became home for a few days, during which time we were subjected to a bombing raid which left us unscathed but damaged HMS *Iron Duke,* a recent arrival.
>
> Almost as traumatic was the Board of Inquiry. There I sat, a 17-year-old boy seaman facing more senior officers than I ever thought existed. They put me at ease immediately and were so kind and sympathetic you wouldn't believe. I suppose it was all the gold braid that initially made me nervous. Shortly after this we were taken to the town of Thurso where we were treated like royalty. I cannot speak highly enough of those wonderful people who gave so much and asked for nothing in return. After a few days we boarded a train at Thurso Station, bound for Portsmouth, which we reached over thirty hours later – what a journey! We did, however, enjoy a wonderful breakfast in Perth and a good late meal in London. Upon arrival at Royal Naval Barracks, Portsmouth, we had a cold meal and a packet of ten cigarettes each – and there were more than 400 of us. Next on the agenda was a really good sleep, after which we were re-kitted and sent on fourteen days survivors' leave.

For U-47, those few days after the attack were spent returning to base, running on the surface at night and lying stationary on the bottom by day. During the long hours of waiting before their attack, a comic had circulated among Prien's crew, the men being particularly amused by the drawing of a bull charging an invisible target with lowered horns and steaming nostrils. When nearly home, Endrass called for a brush and white paint, reproducing the drawing on the conning towers side: so it was that Prien would become known as the 'Bull of Scapa Flow', a symbol of aggressive spirit, an example to all Germans.

As U-47 raced homewards, the crew listened eagerly to news bulletins from the *Grossdeutsche Rundfunk.* British Admiralty reports confirmed that HMS *Royal Oak* had been sunk, 'believed by U-boat action'. As the boat approached Wilhelmshaven on 17 October, a special German broadcast announced that:

> Further to earlier reports of the sinking of the British battleship HMS *Royal Oak,* it is now learnt that the commander of the U-boat, *Kapitänleutnant* Prien, penetrated the strong defences protecting the anchorage of Scapa Flow and torpedoed the ship in harbour during the night. The battleship blew up in a few seconds.

When news of Prien's success was broadcast in Germany there was an absolute frenzy of enthusiasm throughout the Fatherland. U-47 had, effectively, expunged the humiliation of the German High Seas Fleet at Scapa Flow in 1919. U-47 was escorted into Wilhelmshaven by two destroyers and welcomed home by cheering crowds and music. Dönitz himself had travelled especially from Kiel, conferring the Iron Cross 1st Class on Prien and the 2nd Class on the rest of his crew.

U-47 soon left the lock and tied up at its permanent berth. There an officer came aboard and handed Prien, the 'Bull of Scapa Flow', an invitation from Hitler himself for the commander and crew of U-47 to be his guests in Berlin. In the capital, the news spread that Prien and his U-boat heroes had been summoned for an audience with the *Führer,* and when Prien and his men landed at Templehof the airport was packed with people. The radio had announced that Prien's party would travel to the Kaiserhof Hotel, and the route was lined with hysterical crowds, tens of thousands of people, who threw flowers, cigarettes and presents into the open cars as the sailors passed. The hotel itself, where the crew of U-47 was staying, was virtually besieged, the crowd ceaselessly chanting 'We want Prien!' When the crew left the *Kaiserhof* for their audience with Hitler, the crowd actually broke through the police cordon, blocking the street and forcing the submariners to retreat and leave via a back exit.

At the Reich Chancellery, Prien paraded his crew in a large study. Although muted, the cheering crowds could still be heard. Prien himself wrote:

> The adjutant entered and announced the *Führer.* He came in. I had often seen him before, but never had I felt his

greatness as intensely as in this moment … But what was I in comparison with this man, who had felt the degradation of this land on his own, who had dreamed of a freer and happier Fatherland? An unknown man among 80 million he had dreamed then acted. His dream had come true; his acts had forged a new world.

I marched up to the *Führer*. He shook me by the hand and placed the Knight's Cross of the Iron Cross around my neck, honouring the whole crew through me. I felt pride and happiness in this hour; it would be stupid to deny it. But I knew that I stood here, representing the many who, nameless and silent, had fought the same fight … The *Führer* walked along the short line of men, gave everyone his hand and thanked each and every one of them. I walked behind him and looked at them all, man by man, and my heart beat in unison with theirs.

Hitler then made a speech to the crew, mentioning his own experiences under fire in Flanders during the Great War, explained the full significance of their success at Scapa Flow. Prien then reported to Hitler in private before the *Führer* sat down to lunch with the whole crew, who were later taken to the Propaganda Ministry for a tea to which the German press were admitted. Then Prien was the star at a press conference to which both Allied and neutral correspondents were invited. In the evening, U-47's crew were joined at the Wintergarten Theatre by none other than Dr Joseph Goebbels, the Minister of Propaganda himself. The audience cheered, and during the interval Prien had to make a speech. Afterwards the crew were taken on to a nightclub where, in their honour, the ban on dancing had been lifted for that occasion. When asked by a German war correspondent for his impression of the reception in Berlin, the 'Bull of Scapa Flow' replied:

On my arrival I became conscious for the first time of the deep interest the German people had taken in what was, for us U-boat men, a routine voyage. I am convinced that my crew has also been inspired to do everything they can to bring this war to an early, honourable and victorious end.

Günther Prien had become the first U-boat commander of the Second World War to receive the coveted Knight's Cross, which now hung glittering from its red, white and black neck ribbon. While the mood in Germany was completely euphoric, the reverse was true of the effect of U-47's 'routine' sortie on the British.

At the stunned Scapa Flow, confusion and speculation remained rife about the sinking of HMS *Royal Oak.* Although the ship's captain, Captain William Benn, was convinced he had been torpedoed, the only way to be sure was for divers to examine the wreck, so Sandy Robertson, a local commercial salvage diver, was sent for from his cottage on Hoy at 3 am. At daylight out in the anchorage, lying in just 32 metres of water, the hull of the sunken battleship could be clearly seen. Robertson's task was grim, hundreds of bodies lay scattered on the seabed, and he found three big holes in the ship's hull. Then he found the crucial piece of evidence: the propeller of one of Prien's torpedoes. Once salvaged, there was no more argument: incredible though it seemed and painful as it was to admit, the enemy had achieved the impossible and penetrated the anchorage's 'impregnable' defences with a submarine and torpedoed *Royal Oak.* Not only that, but the belligerent vessel had also escaped, completely unscathed and undetected.

The fate of *Royal Oak* was released to the British people the same day. Coming so soon after the *Courageous* disaster, it was an absolutely shattering blow to British national pride and morale – especially given that the ship had been lost within Scapa Flow. The nation just could not understand how this tragedy had happened. Most of the ship's company were from Portsmouth and Devonport, and in those areas families were desperate for news of their loved ones; they would have to wait several days before lists of survivors were available and published accordingly.

On 17 October, the First Lord of the Admiralty, Winston Churchill, spoke in the House of Commons about the disaster. While it was accepted that a

U-boat was responsible, Churchill commented that it remained 'a matter of conjecture' as to how the submarine had penetrated the defences, given that throughout the Great War 'the anchorage had remained immune from such attack, on the account of the obstacles imposed by the currents and net barrages'. Paying tribute to Prien's feat of arms, Churchill said 'this entry by a U-boat must be considered as a remarkable exploit of professional skill and daring'. Although officially he described it as 'a regrettable tragedy', Churchill impressed the fact that the loss of *Royal Oak* would have no bearing on the overall war at sea; inwardly, however, the First Sea Lord was deeply saddened by the loss *of Royal Oak*.

Naturally a Board of Inquiry was immediately convened, which heard testimonies from numerous witnesses and went through the whole business with a very fine-tooth comb. No evidence was obtained that a submarine had either entered or left the flow, and nor was there any indication that a U-boat had been destroyed in the anchorage. The Board agreed, however, that the experience of survivors (no doubt supported by Robertson's discovery of the torpedo component) suggested that the *Royal Oak* had been hit by torpedoes, and one witness, Marine Owens, Bandmaster 2nd Class, had imparted a crucial eyewitness account:

> I went over [the side of the ship] with another person, I think an officer. He was wearing pyjamas and was very tall. After we got 300 yards from the ship we trod water to have a rest. He then said 'Hello, do you see that over there?' I looked in the direction he pointed and distinctly saw the conning tower of a submarine some 200 [*sic*] yards away. The submarine was on the starboard quarter of the *Royal Oak* and appeared to be stationary. After that I said to my companion we had better make for the drifter, which was lying some 400 yards to port of the *Royal Oak*. We swam towards the drifter. I then missed my companion and have been unable to trace him since. I am absolutely certain I saw the conning tower of a submarine from my position in the water. I have not the slightest doubt whatever.

Owens was considered a first-class witness and his testimony was accepted.

Having confirmed that a U-boat was indeed responsible, the Board of Inquiry also considered the state of Scapa Flow's defences, which were clearly inadequate, concluding that they required 'reconsideration' to include patrol vessels, ASDIC defences, minefields, the complete blocking of the eastern entrances (where U-47 had sneaked through), lookouts, guns, searchlights, and the extension of boom nets as close to the seabed as was practical. In all, eleven possible weak spots were found at which a U-boat could have entered Scapa Flow – hardly an impressive scenario and one which laid blame for the tragedy firmly on the Admiralty, which naturally blamed the senior officer on the spot, Admiral Sir Wilfred French, ACOS, who was retired. This was unfair; before the war, French had warned his Commander-in-Chief that he would be willing to take a destroyer, much less a submarine, through Kirk Sound in the right conditions; no heed was taken of this warning. Blaming French was clearly an extremely unjust decision, and probably a political one.

A sub-committee was set up to research the defensive situation, concluding that blockships were insufficient to seal off the entrances to Scapa Flow. Instead, it was decided to construct concrete causeways, called 'Churchill Barriers', between the islands concerned. In due course these were built by Italian prisoners of war, who also left behind a somewhat more artistic cultural legacy: a superb chapel built in a prefabricated hut on Lamb Holm (and which can be visited today). Although the barriers were not entirely completed until 1944, the Germans never tried to venture within the lion's den again.

What Prien's victory did do for the *Kriegsmarine* was not only to exorcise the ghosts of the Kaiser's navy's defeat in 1918, and the consequent 'Grand Scuttle' in 1919, but also to increase Hitler's confidence in the *U-bootwaffe*. Indeed, straightaway the *Führer* lifted the existing restrictions on U-boat operations: all enemy ships, including liners in convoy, would be attacked on sight. For the first time, the whole nation embraced the idea that the hated Royal Navy could be defeated. As a result of Prien's success, Dönitz was promoted to Rear-Admiral and Commander-in-Chief of U-boats.

FACES OF HMS ROYAL OAK

He had proved the worth of the submarine, and was now in a position to actually put his 'Wolf Pack' theories into practice. As Churchill, who in 1940 became Prime Minister of wartime Britain, wrote after the war: 'It was only the U-boat menace that ever really worried me,' – and the *Royal Oak* tragedy had proven early on just what an audacious U-boat commander could achieve.

Typically, military history is written from the top down. Survivors often left behind written or recorded memoirs, unique first-hand accounts adding the human experience and colour to the stark official records and facts. Those who perished, however, have no voice, and are very much a matter of 'hidden history'. In this unique book on HMS *Royal Oak* we are approaching the subject in the main from the bottom up – revealing the faces of casualties, and in some cases last letters home and associated artefacts, shared with us by their families and friends. The loss of HMS *Royal Oak* was a disaster, and a personal tragedy for the families of 835 sailors. It is entirely right that they be remembered in this way, so in many ways this book is a memorial to their sacrifice.

HMS *Royal Oak* in 1939, shortly before being sunk at anchor in Scapa Flow. Of great interest in this photograph is the starboard torpedo blister, a recently added modification which actually contributed to the aged battleship's tragic fate. (Orkney Library & Archive)

FACES OF HMS ROYAL OAK

Above: The fourth of her class, HMS *Royal Oak* was laid down at Devonport Dockyard in January 1914. Completed in 1916, *Royal Oak* first saw action at the Battle of Jutland. (Historic Military Press)

Right: A superb study of HMS *Royal Oak*'s forward gun turrets and bridge, the sailors on deck providing a sense of proportion. (Orkney Library & Archive)

FACES OF HMS ROYAL OAK

HMS *Royal Oak* at full steam and turning at speed in the Pentland Firth. (Orkney Library & Archive)

HMS *Royal Oak* firing her 6-inch and 15-inch guns during the First World War. (National Museum of the US Navy)

FACES OF HMS ROYAL OAK

Above: Mail day on the lower deck on board HMS *Royal Oak* during the First World War. (National Museum of the US Navy)

Right: Gunners manning one of HMS *Royal Oak*'s anti-aircraft guns during the First World War. (National Museum of the US Navy)

FACES OF HMS ROYAL OAK

HMS *Royal Oak* towing a destroyer during the First World War. (Library of Congress)

HMS *Royal Oak* taking a destroyer in tow during the First World War. (Dutch National Archives)

FACES OF HMS ROYAL OAK

HMS *Royal Oak* wreathed in gunsmoke during practice firing in the Pentland Firth. (Orkney Library & Archive)

HMS *Royal Oak*, port view. (Orkney Library & Archive)

FACES OF HMS ROYAL OAK

HMS *Royal Oak* at gunnery practice. (Orkney Library & Archive)

FACES OF HMS ROYAL OAK

The forward gun turrets of HMS *Royal Oak* in freezing conditions.

'Fire!'

Training on one of the ship's anti-aircraft guns.

FACES OF HMS ROYAL OAK

Left: A torpedo being loaded aboard.

Below: HMS *Royal Oak*, veteran of the Battle of Jutland.

FACES OF HMS ROYAL OAK

HMS *Royal Oak* steaming into Scapa Flow.

HMS *Royal Oak* passing Nelson's flagship, HMS *Victory*, at Portsmouth.

The catapult fitted in 1934 to the roof of 'X' turret to accommodate launching a de Havilland seaplane, used for aerial reconnaissance, which was recovered to the ship via a crane.

FACES OF HMS ROYAL OAK

Right: A view of part of HMS *Royal Oak*'s superstructure. (National Museum of the US Navy)

Below: A view of the Royal Navy battleship HMS *Royal Oak*. (Historic Military Press)

FACES OF HMS ROYAL OAK

Captain Willian Benn, captain of HMS *Royal Oak*. He would survive the sinking of his ship by U-47, only leaving when *Royal Oak* sank beneath him. The Admiralty concluded that Benn had acted in the 'best traditions of the service'.

The drifter *Daisy II*: for the skipper of which, John Gatt, and his crew, no praise could high enough regarding their efforts to rescue survivors.

A formal photograph of a division of the ship's company.

The once proud Imperial German High Seas Fleet interned at Scapa Flow after the First World War's Armistice – and before the ships were scuttled by the crews on Midsummer's Day, 1919.

Opposite: First World War U-boat veteran and submarine warfare expert, *Kommodore* Karl Dönitz – who began planning the 'boldest of bold enterprises': to get a U-Boat into Scapa Flow, to wreak havoc among the Royal Navy's Home Fleet before safely slipping away.

FACES OF HMS ROYAL OAK

FACES OF HMS ROYAL OAK

The *Kriegsmarine* (German Navy) was forbidden submarines under the provisions of the Versailles Peace Settlement of 1919 – but after the Nazis came to power in 1933, the *Diktat* was increasingly rejected. Here, the *Führer*, Adolf Hitler, inspects a small coastal U-boat, a Type IIB, before the Second World War.

A Type VIIB U-boat, identical to U-47 – which would send HMS *Royal Oak* to the bottom of Scapa Flow on the night of 13/14 October 1939.

FACES OF HMS ROYAL OAK

Kapitänleutnant Günther Prien, the commander of U-47, chosen by Dönitz to undertake the 'boldest of bold enterprises' and penetrate Scapa Flow.

FACES OF HMS ROYAL OAK

Opposite: From the album of U-boat commander Herbert Bruninghaus, a torpedo being winched aboard a Type VII.

U-boat men guide the 'eel' into their submarine's magazine.

Engelbert Endrass, Prien's second in command aboard U-47; he later had his own command and became highly decorated before his boat, U-576, was lost with all hands north-east of the Azores on 21 December 1941.

FACES OF HMS ROYAL OAK

Above: The only vessel to the north of *Royal Oak* at Scapa Flow at the time of Prien's attack was the seaplane carrier HMS *Pegasus*. Commissioned in 1914 as *Ark Royal*, she was renamed *Pegasus* in 1934 when the famous name was to be used for a new fleet carrier. (USNHHC)

Below: U-47 hit HMS *Royal Oak* with four torpedoes, this being the propulsion unit of one, recovered by divers shortly after the event and proving beyond doubt that a German submarine was responsible. Today, the artefact is preserved by and can be seen at Stromness Museum, Orkney.

FACES OF HMS ROYAL OAK

Above and below: After the 'boldest of bold enterprises', U-47 returned safely to Wilhelmshaven and a hero's welcome.

Prien, in this posed photograph, revelling in the huge publicity surrounding his success – as a result of which he became known as the 'Bull of Scapa Flow', and hence the cartoon on his conning tower.

FACES OF HMS ROYAL OAK

Left: The crew of U-47 travelling to their audience with Hitler in Berlin, with thousands of people lining the route and sharing in their moment of triumph.

Below: U-47 had in four torpedoes expunged the shame of 1919 – and clearly these ecstatic Berliners revelled in the sweetness of their revenge against the Royal Navy.

Hitler invests Prien with the coveted *Ritterkruez*, the Knight's Cross of the Iron Cross.

FACES OF HMS ROYAL OAK

Hitler dining with U-47's officers and men at the Reich Chancellery.

Opposite: The victorious Prien, now a household name in Germany and beyond, returning by train to Wilhelmshaven after the triumphal celebrations. Ultimately, Prien and U-47 would be lost, with all hands, near the Rockall Banks on 7 March 1941.

FACES OF HMS ROYAL OAK

FACES OF HMS ROYAL OAK

Above: Having returned from a War Patrol, *Kapitänleutnant* Günther Prien is pictured here in conversation with three Luftwaffe airmen who were rescued by U-47 after their aircraft, a Dornier Do 18, ditched in the North Sea on 6 June 1940. (National Museum of Denmark)

Below: Taken during the celebratory sailing around Kiel harbour on 23 October 1939, this famous photograph of U-47 shows the crew of the battleship *Scharnhorst* parading along the edge of the deck in honour of the U-boat crew's daring penetration of Scapa Flow. (USNHHC)

FACES OF HMS ROYAL OAK

A picture of *Kapitänleutnant* Günther Prien on his return from a War Patrol. (Bundesarchiv 183-2006-1130-500/CC BY-SA 3.0)

FACES OF HMS ROYAL OAK

Above: A view of U-47 photographed from or near the battleship *Scharnhorst* circa late 1939 or early 1940. The original caption states that this submarine was returning to Kiel, Germany, from a War Patrol. Note insignia on the conning tower, which looks very much like *U-47*'s 'Bull of Scapa Flow' emblem. (USNHHC)

Opposite above: The crew of U-47 greeted by adoring members of the Bund Deutscher Mädel, the 'BDM', the female equivalent of the Nazi Hitler Youth for boys.

Opposite below: With the sinking of HMS *Royal Oak*, Prien became Nazi Germany's first celebrated hero of the war against Britain – this being a signed souvenir card. (Ian Sayer Archive)

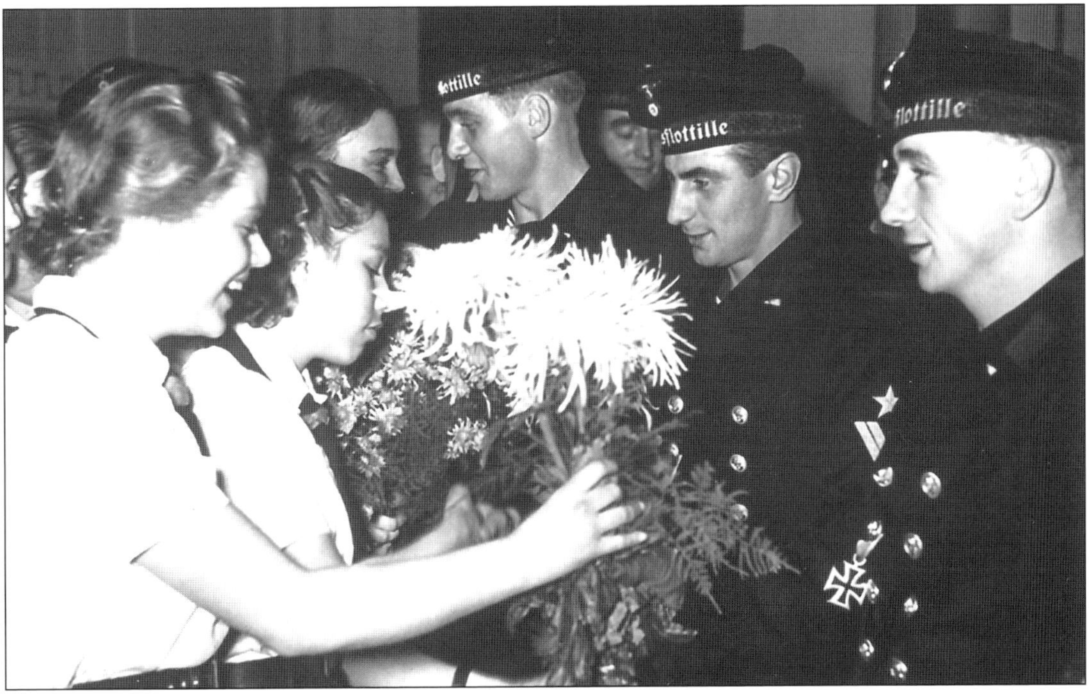

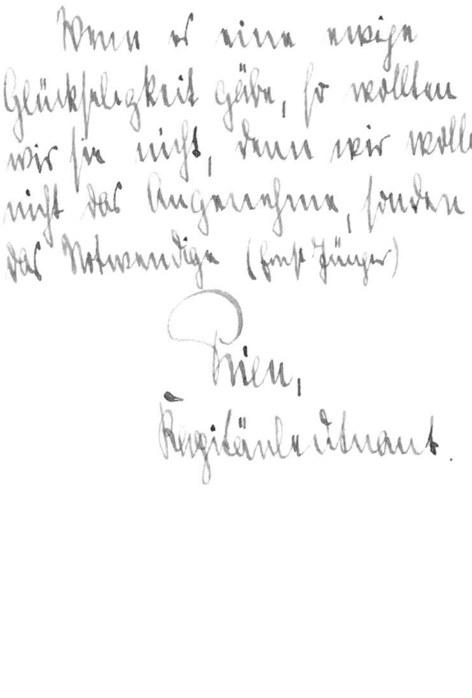
Wenn es eine ewige Glückseligkeit gäbe, so wollten wir sie nicht, denn wir wollen nicht das Angenehme, sondern das Notwendige (Ernst Jünger)

Prien,
Kapitänleutnant.

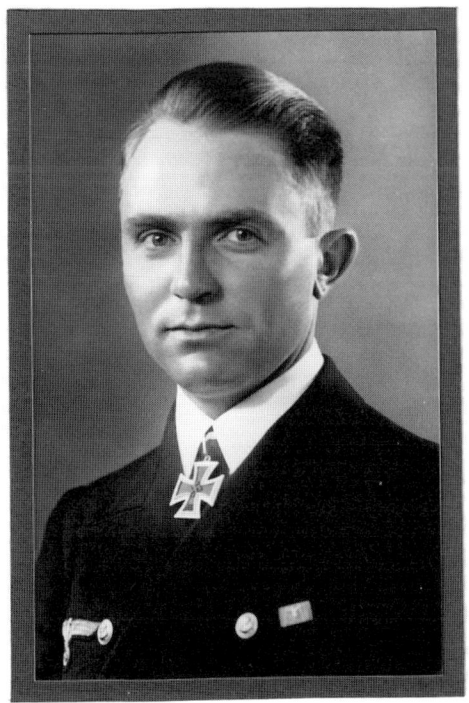

FACES OF HMS ROYAL OAK

Above: The crew of U-47 also became revered heroes in Germany, this being a souvenir card signed by them. (Ian Sayer Archive)

Left: In 1958, surprisingly soon after the war, Harald Reinl directed a German film produced by Gero Weckler based on Prien's life, U-47: *Kapitänleutnant* Prien, starring Dieter Eppler, this being the film poster.

Opposite above: Promotional material for the 1948 film. (Ian Sayer Archive)

Opposite below: Another item of the promotional material produced for the 1948 film. (Ian Sayer Archive)

FACES OF HMS ROYAL OAK

After the horse, or more accurately U-47, had bolted, the Admiralty ordered construction of the Churchill Barrier, constructed by Italian prisoners of war from concrete blocks, between Glim Holm and Lamp Holm, thereby blocking the access into Scapa Flow and thus preventing a repetition of the HMS *Royal Oak* disaster.

Part II

The Photographs

Above, opposite and overleaf: Relatives outside the Portsmouth Naval Dockyard anxiously hoping for news of survivors from the sinking of HMS *Royal Oak*.

FACES OF HMS ROYAL OAK

FACES OF HMS ROYAL OAK

Petty Officer Henry George Attfield, a 33-year-old married man among those who perished aboard HMS *Royal Oak*. (Linda Warren)

FACES OF HMS ROYAL OAK

Henry Attfield (left) and pals. (Linda Warren)

Happier times: Henry Attfield and wife, Alice. (Linda Warren)

14 of October 1939

Dear Colin,

Thank you ever so much for your very welcome letter which I received on Saturday the 7th of October.

So pleased to know you received the Postal Order quite safely, and I will send you another one later on.

Please take care of mummy for me, won't you? and I think you are very lucky to have Evelyn talking to you now.

I must close now, Colin old chap, so hoping to see you soon, I will close with fondest Love and Kisses

From, Your Ever
Loving
Daddy.

x x x x x x x x x
x x x x x x x x
x x x x x
x x x
x

Petty Officer Attfield's last letter home, to his son, Colin, is dated 14 October 1939 – the very date HMS *Royal Oak* sank. (Linda Warren)

FACES OF HMS ROYAL OAK

Petty Officer Attfield's children Colin and Evelyn – sadly their father was not among the survivors, whose names were posted up outside the Portsmouth Dockyard, but was among the missing. (Linda Attfield)

This scroll commemorates
Petty Officer H. G. Attfield
Royal Navy
held in honour as one who served King and Country in the world war of 1939-1945 and gave his life to save mankind from tyranny. May his sacrifice help to bring the peace and freedom for which he died.

The official scroll commemorating Petty Officer Attfield, who is remembered on Panel 33, Column 1, of the Portsmouth Naval Memorial.

FACES OF HMS ROYAL OAK

Margaret Hothi was 2 when her father, Petty Officer Frederick Charles Bealing, perished aboard *Royal Oak*. Naturally Margaret has no recollections, but her elder sister, Doris, accompanied their mother, Elsie, to the Portsmouth Dockyard, anxious for news – but Petty Officer Bealing had not survived and is also commemorated on Panel 33, Column 1, of the Portsmouth Naval Memorial.

FACES OF HMS ROYAL OAK

Leading Stoker James Bailey Fisher, pictured here upon his marriage to Doris, was reported missing, aged 31, and is remembered on Panel 35, Column 1 of the Portsmouth Naval Memorial. (Mick Fisher)

A card sent home by Leading Stoker Fisher. (Mick Fisher)

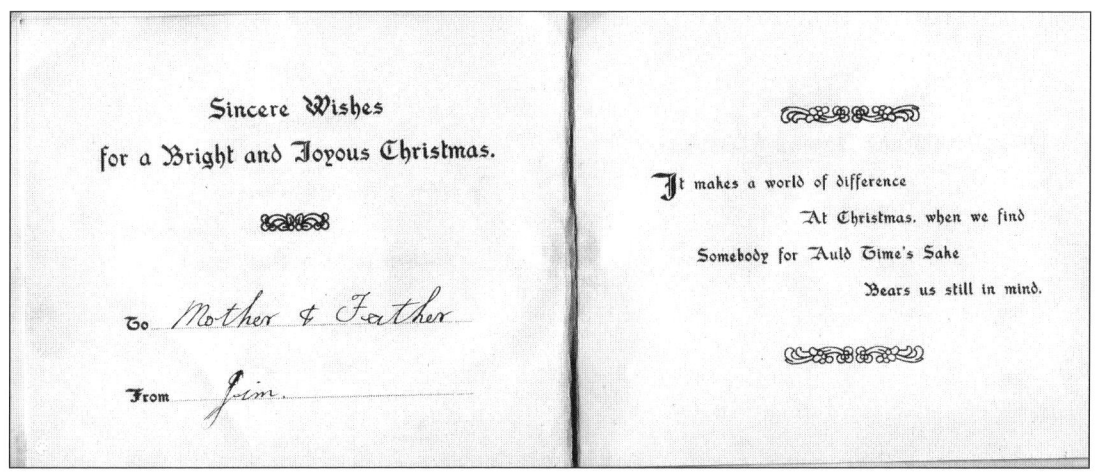

The last Christmas card sent home by Leading Stoker Fisher, to his parents, James and Margaret Fisher, of Cosham, Hampshire. (Mick Fisher)

FACES OF HMS ROYAL OAK

Able Seaman Thomas Chadwick, from Oldham, pictured with his wife, Rose, had first served as a cabin boy in the Royal Navy, joining in 1914 and serving throughout the First World War. Afterwards he joined the reserve and became a Stoker (Engineering) in the 1920s, re-enlisting in the Royal Navy when the Second World War broke out. Chadwick, another father, sadly went down with the ship and is remembered on Panel 33, Column 2, of the Portsmouth Naval Memorial. (Steven W Chadwick)

Many of the ship's company were boy sailors, among them Boy 1st Class William Henry Clacher – lost aged 16, remembered on Panel 34, Column 2, of the Portsmouth Naval Memorial. William is seen here (left) with a pal while training at the shore-based HMS *Vincent*. (Paul Clacher)

The telegram informing William Clacher's parents that their son was missing. On 25 May 1940, William's father, Battery Sergeant Major H. Clacher of the Royal Artillery, was reported missing while fighting with the British Expeditionary Force in France; thankfully lightning did not strike twice on this occasion, and he returned home safely via Dunkirk. (Paul Clacher)

Opposite: The official condolence card from Buckingham Palace received by William Clacher's bereaved parents. (Paul Clacher)

BUCKINGHAM PALACE

The Queen and I offer you our heartfelt sympathy in your great sorrow.

We pray that your country's gratitude for a life so nobly given in its service may bring you some measure of consolation.

George R.I.

Mrs. Mary Clacher.

FACES OF HMS ROYAL OAK

FACES OF HMS ROYAL OAK

Opposite: Jack Cundall was the *Royal Oak*'s Paymaster Captain, and spent the early hours of his 48th birthday, 14 October 1939, in the sea having abandoned ship. Missed by the first pass of the *Daisy II*, Jack was later rescued. (Cherry Conway-Hughes)

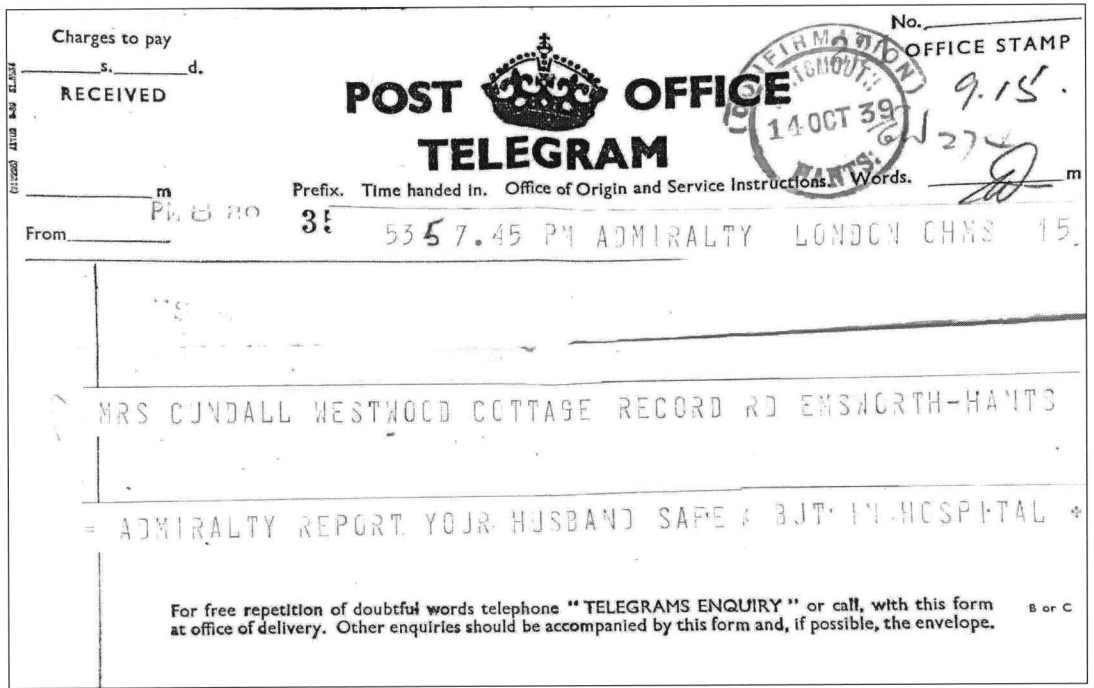

The telegram to Mrs Cundall, reporting her husband, Jack, to be safe. (Cherry Conway-Hughes)

FACES OF HMS ROYAL OAK

Petty Officer Victor Cruse, pictured here in 1938, was also among the lucky survivors – his daughter was born six days after the ship went down. (Jean Westerman)

FACES OF HMS ROYAL OAK

Ordinary Seaman Cuthbert Heslop, of Stockton-on-Tees, was a swimming champion in his home town – but lost his life when *Royal Oak* went down. The third of seven children, he was 18, and is remembered on Panel 34, Column 1 of the Portsmouth Naval Memorial. (Susan Heslop)

Cuthbert Heslop's cap tally from training aboard HMS *Victory*. (Susan Heslop)

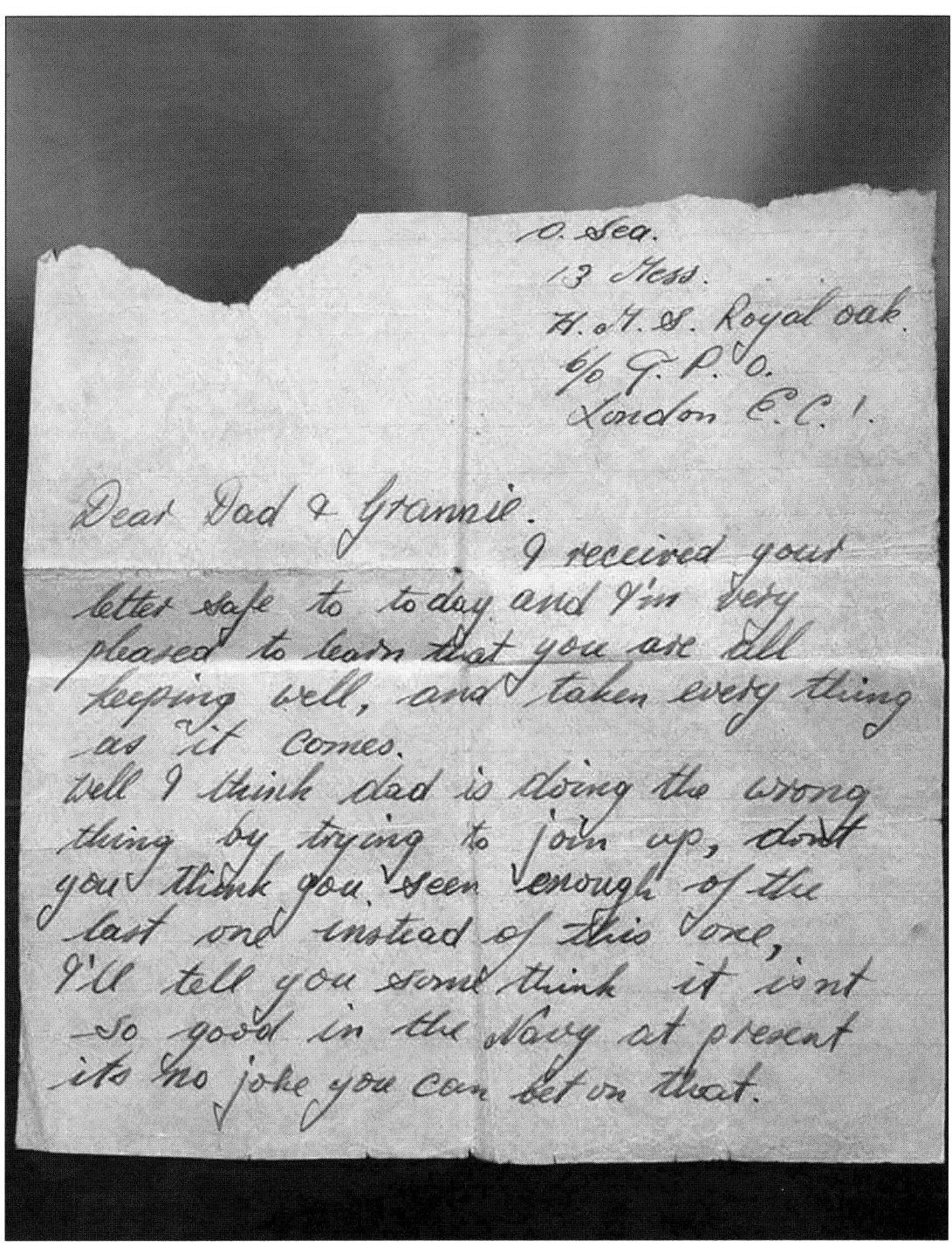

Above and overleaf: Cuthbert Heslop's last letter home. (Susan Heslop)

so. I think you wont to stop at home and be a lot safer thats you would on these ships. I only wish I was home at present, I bet there's tons of money to be made.

I had a letter from alf and he is at the Isle of Man, and he sayes he is haveing a good time. I dont no when we are comming on leave but I dont think it will before christmas.

I think I've told you all for now so I say cheerio hoping you like my photo, which I had took aboard.

So I'll wish you all the best of luck hoping to see you all soon. Good bye and good luck.

Love lily. Cuthbert xxxx

Chief Stoker Ernest William Farr was 38 when lost with *Royal Oak*; he had previously served aboard HMS *Hood*, sunk by the infamous *Bismarck* in 1941. Married to Elizabeth with a young son, Gordon, he is remembered on Panel 35, Column 1 of the Portsmouth Naval Memorial. (Graham Farr)

FACES OF HMS ROYAL OAK

Chief Stoker Farr's medals, from left: 1939–45 Star, War Medal and the Atlantic Star. (Graham Farr)

Opposite: Also remembered on Panel 35, Column 1 of the Portsmouth Naval Memorial is Leading Stoker Henry Sidney Huggins, who was lost aged 28 and pictured here at a happier occasion. (Roy Ingham)

FACES OF HMS ROYAL OAK

FACES OF HMS ROYAL OAK

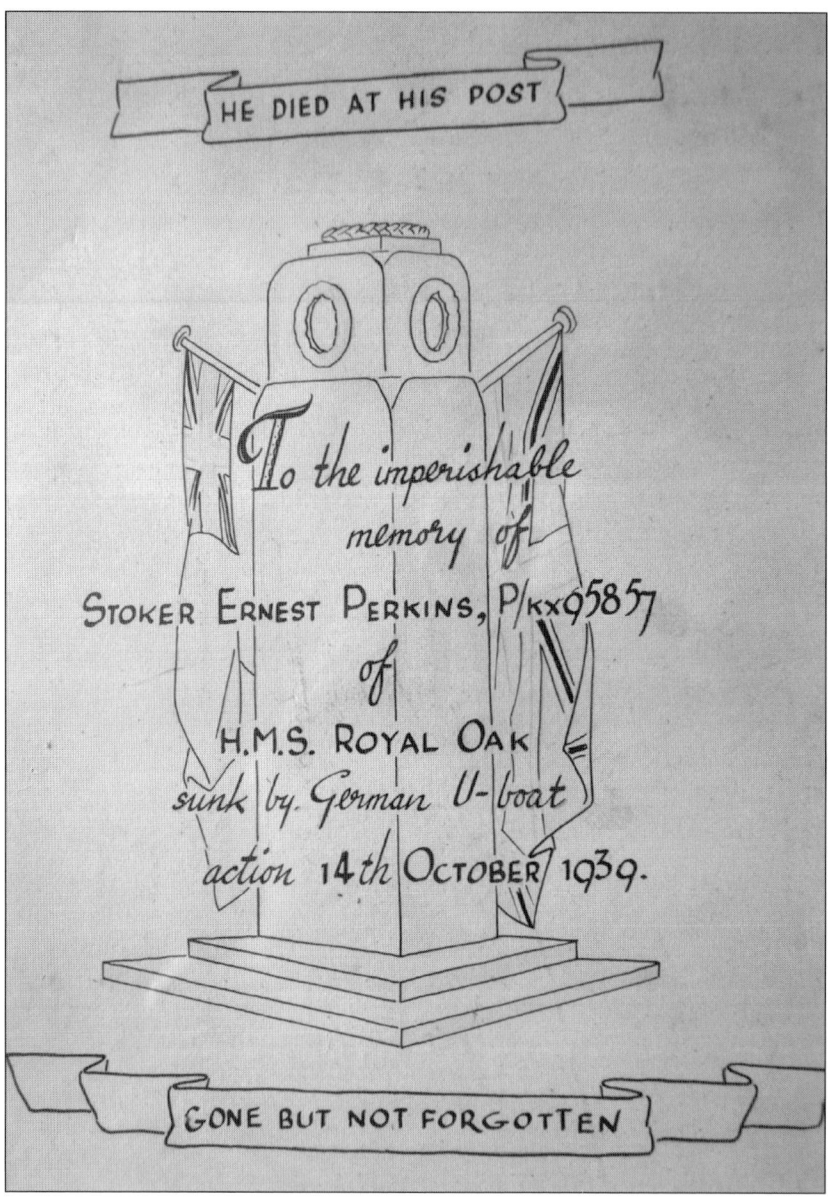

Sadly, the likeness of Stoker 2nd Class Ernest Edward Perkins, remembered on Panel 35, Column 2 of the Portsmouth Naval Memorial, has been lost to the living record, no photographs of him having apparently survived. This is a commemorative card which Jim Perkins remembers always being beside his grandmother's bed, with his lost uncle's HMS *Royal Oak* cap tally hung over a corner – which the bereaved mother was ultimately buried with. Ernest's younger brother's birthday, coincidentally, was 14 October, so the boys' parents were in the unenviable position of remembering the death of one while celebrating birth of another. (Jim Perkins)

Frank Rann was born in Newport, on the Isle of Wight, on 26 July 1905, entering Boy Service with the Royal Navy in 1921. On 28 July 1938, Rann was awarded the Long Service and Good Conduct Medal, by which time he also had three Good Conduct badges. Between the wars he served on many ships, notably HMS *Hood* and HMS *Revenge*. On 21 January 1939, he was posted to HMS *Royal Oak*, and promoted to Chief Petty Officer aboard on 31 May 1939. Chief Petty Officer went down with the ship and is remembered on Panel 33, Column 1, of the Portsmouth Naval Memorial. (Peter Gisborne)

[Telegram reproduction:]

POST OFFICE TELEGRAM

Received 8.30 a.m.

Prefix 1.5 Office of Origin: Portsmouth OHMS Words: 32

Office Stamp: HAVANT 16 OC 39

Mrs Jessie Rann 6 Coastguard Houses Langstone Havant.

Deeply regret to report death of your husband Frank Rann Chief Petty Officer Official Number J100664 on war service = Rear Admiral RN Barracks Portsmouth

The pencil-written telegram informing Chief Petty Officer Rann's widow, Marjorie, of his death.

Opposite: Rear-Admiral Lait's letter of condolence to Mrs Rann – he would sign many such that fateful day. Left alone to raise two small children, when the spirited Mrs Rann received her husband's medals in 1951, she threw them straight in the bin, saying 'I can't feed hungry children on them!'. (Peter Gisborne)

Royal Naval Barracks,
PORTSMOUTH.
14th October, 1939.

Dear Madam,

It is with very deep regret that I learn of the sad death of your husband Frank Rann, Chief Petty Officer, J.100664.

Please allow me to express the sincere sympathy of the officers and men of the Royal Navy.

Yours faithfully,

C. Lait

REAR ADMIRAL.

Mrs. J. Rann,
   8 Coastguard Houses,
     Langstone, Havant.

Able Seaman Stanley Cole was among those luckily rescued from the cold sea by *Daisy II*. (Mary Cole)

FACES OF HMS ROYAL OAK

Many years after the sinking, Stanley Cole (left) got to meet and shake the hand of Johnny Duthie (right), skipper of the *Daisy II*. (Mary Cole)

The likeness of 20-year-old Supply Assistant Hubert John Cousins has apparently also been lost to the living record; he too went down with the ship and is remembered on Panel 35, Column 3, of the Portsmouth Naval Memorial. This, however, is his HMS *Royal Oak* cap tally. (Ralph Cousins)

Also lost was Boy 1st Class Frederick Marshall, who had only joined the ship a few days previously. Frederick is pictured here (left) with his father, Jim Stoker, and younger cousin Alan Stoker, outside the family business, Stoker's Shop in Bridge Street, Morpeth, Northumberland. (Gordon Stoker)

Opposite: 18-year-old Frederick Marshall's last scribbled letter home; he is remembered on Panel 34, Column 3, of the Portsmouth Naval Memorial. (Gordon Stoker)

Y.M.C.A.
WITH HIS MAJESTY'S FORCES

PLEASE ADDRESS YOUR REPLY TO

No. _____ Rank _____ Name _____
Address _____

Thursday. Date _____

Dear Pop,

Sorry I didn't write you sooner. Have been on the "Hawkins" am going up to Scapa Flow to-day. Am writing from London. It will break my heart to pass through MORPETH.

Fred.

FACES OF HMS ROYAL OAK

Stoker Cecil J. Lucking survived the sinking of HMS *Royal Oak* but was sadly lost on HMS *Porpoise* in the Far East on 19 January 1945, the last Royal Navy submarine lost to enemy action; he is remembered on Panel 89, Column 3 of the Portsmouth Naval Memorial. (Iain Rant)

A report appearing in the *Jersey Evening Post* reporting on three Channel Islanders lost with HMS *Royal Oak*: Able Seaman Cecil Watts, Boy 1st Class Denis Patch, and Petty Officer W.P. Adams. (Julie Bisson)

FACES OF HMS ROYAL OAK

Denis Patch while training at HMS *Vincent* in 1938. (Julie Bisson)

FACES OF HMS ROYAL OAK

Denis Patch (left) with an unknown comrade aboard HMS *Royal Oak* – note cap tallies. (Julie Bisson)

> Sunday,
> 8/10/39
>
> Dear Mum
>
> I thought Eileen had grown up a bit. I see she still needs somebody at home to look after her, somebody with a strong hand, what do you think about it? What did Uncle Frank ⟨⟩ volunteer for? I bet his wife will be upset, how are his twins getting on, when I showed the boys the photograph I had taken with them, they did not half pull my leg about it. I did think my lucky stars that I was born with a thick skin. Have see some rotten weather lately rain and blowing a gale with the seas like mountains. What sort of weather are you experiencing at Jersey. I don't suppose there is any visitors left now. Well I am afraid am going to break my resolution by asking you for a £1 to go ashore with, for during this war we are not sure of regular payment. Hope all is well at home everybody well, how is Marjorie progressing at school. I bet she is a pretty clever kid now, give her my love.
>
> yours ever
> Denis
> xxxxxxxx

Denis Patch's last letter home; he is remembered on Panel 34, Column 2 of the Portsmouth Naval Memorial. (Julie Bisson)

FACES OF HMS ROYAL OAK

Also lost was Petty Officer Robert George Puddy, known by his family as 'George'. (Catherine Renouf)

Petty Officer Puddy was survived by his wife, Mary, and their young daughter, Dawn. From Northwood on the Isle of Wight, this memorial in the church there remembers George, in whose memory family members still light candles there. (Catherine Renouf)

Opposite: Another lost soul that fateful night in the autumn of 1939 was Petty Officer W.D. 'Bill' Royal, an engine room artificer, remembered on Panel 34, Column 3 of the Portsmouth Naval Memorial. (Steve Wales)

FACES OF HMS ROYAL OAK

Among the first fifteen survivors rescued from the sea was 17-year-old Boy 1st Class Edward 'Ted' Scovell, who later served aboard HMS *Penelope*, ultimately surviving the war to become a Commissioned Gunner at HMS *Ganges* post-war. (Kieran Ellix)

Among the Royal Marines lost with the ship was 22-year-old Marine Verdun Loos James Pierpoint, who had enlisted at Southampton in 1934; he is commemorated on Panel 91 of the Portsmouth Naval Memorial. (Tania Bolton)

FACES OF HMS ROYAL OAK

Leading Stoker Frederick Walker, from Rotherham, had been a sailor for twelve years when he lost his life on 14 October 1939, aged 33; he is remembered on Panel 35, Column 1, of the Portsmouth Naval Memorial. (Julia Barker)

Above: Frederick Walker was a married man, his wife, Doris, having set up home in Portchester, seen here with her husband and their daughter, Patricia; their second child was born a few days after Frederick's death. (Julia Barker)

Right: Frederick Walker joined HMS *Royal Oak* in June 1939, to serve alongside his brother-in-law, Stoker 1st Class Walter James Hawkins, who also lost his life that October night – so Doris Walker lost both her husband and brother to the torpedoes of U-47. Walter is also remembered on Panel 35, Column 1, of the Portsmouth Naval Memorial. (Julia Barker)

FACES OF HMS ROYAL OAK

Leading Seaman Edward Benjamin Warriner came from landlocked Cirencester in Gloucestershire, and joined the Royal Navy against his father's wishes. He was 29 when reported missing after HMS *Royal Oak* sank, and is remembered on Panel 33, Column 2, of the Portsmouth Naval Memorial. (Malcolm Warriner)

FACES OF HMS ROYAL OAK

Able Seaman James Lawrence Wormald was the 38-year-old husband of the expectant Rosie Annie Wormald of Weymouth, Dorset, and he too remains missing from the sinking. Remembered on Panel 33, Column 3, of the Portsmouth Naval Memorial, James and Rosie's son, Tony, was born in February 1940. (Tony Royal Wormald)

FACES OF HMS ROYAL OAK

All we know of Boy 1st Class Francis William Annell is that he was the foster-son of James and Elsie Cole, of Caversham, Oxford, and he was 17 when reported missing on 14 October 1939; he is remembered on Panel 34, Column 1, of the Portsmouth Naval Memorial. (via survivor, the late Bert Pocock)

Also 17 was Boy 1st Class Roland Arno, from County Durham, remembered on Panel 34, Column 1, of the Portsmouth Naval Memorial. (Doris Leek)

Supply Assistant Arthur Edward Bargery, a Welshman from Roath, Cardiff, was 20 when he lost his life in Scapa Flow that fateful night; remembered on Panel 35, Column 3, of the Portsmouth Naval Memorial. (Margaret Warburton)

FACES OF HMS ROYAL OAK

All we know of 21-year old Able Seaman Harold Brown is that he was the son of Ellen Brown, of Derby, and is remembered on Panel 33, Column 2, of the Portsmouth Naval Memorial

FACES OF HMS ROYAL OAK

Having previously served on HMS *Vernon*, Leading Stoker William Edward Chesman was 27 when he went down with *Royal Oak*. On 2 April 1938, he had married Barbara Joan Adams, the couple subsequently having two sons, Peter William and Edward Charles. Remembered on Panel 35, Column 1, of the Portsmouth Naval Memorial. (Rachel Chesman)

FACES OF HMS ROYAL OAK

Boy 1st Class Harry Griffin, from Walsall, Staffordshire, was the third of six children and the eldest son, whose father was killed in a mining accident during 1937. He was 17 when lost with *Royal Oak* and is remembered on Panel 34, Column 2, of the Portsmouth Naval Memorial. (Joan Hathaway)

FACES OF HMS ROYAL OAK

Bandmaster (Royal Marines) Arthur Golding (extreme left), parading in Kirkwall, Orkney, a few hours before he lost his life aboard HMS *Royal Oak*; he was 35 and is remembered on Panel 36, Column 2, of the Portsmouth Naval Memorial. (Brian Otway)

Arthur Golding's wife, Dorothy, like countless others, became a war widow facing an uphill struggle. (Brian Otway)

FACES OF HMS ROYAL OAK

Above: Dorothy Golding died aged 94 in 1999; on 14 October 2000, her nephew, Brian Otway, joined Royal Navy divers on their annual visit to the wreck of HMS *Royal Oak*, wherein he interred his late aunt's ashes, thus reuniting her with Arthur on the 61st anniversary of the sinking. (Brian Otway)

Left: Another Marine lost was Kenneth Edwin Hall, a 19-year-old from Reading, whose father served in the Royal Marines at Gallipoli aboard HMS *Glory*. Remembered on Panel 36, Column 1, of the Portsmouth Naval Memorial. (Shirley Bird)

FACES OF HMS ROYAL OAK

Marine Charles Frederick Hemsley came from Sheffield, and is remembered on Panel 36, Column 1, of the Portsmouth Naval Memorial. (Kathryn Trower)

FACES OF HMS ROYAL OAK

Boy 1st Class John Francis Humber was only 16 when he too went down with the ship. From a farming family, John's mother was killed on 13 October 1935, when she was hit by a car in Ashington, West Sussex, while out cycling with him. John's sister, Helena, died aged 5, on 14 August 1935. With *Royal Oak* being sunk on the night of 13/14 October 1939, unsurprisingly the Humber family always considered the thirteenth and fourteenth days of each month potentially unlucky. John is remembered on Panel 34, Column 2, of the Portsmouth Naval Memorial. (Paul Humber)

FACES OF HMS ROYAL OAK

Boy 1st Class Herbert Henry Hixon was only 16 when he too perished with HMS *Royal Oak*; from Swanage, Dorset, he is remembered on Panel 34, Column 2, of the Portsmouth Naval Memorial. (via survivor, the late Bert Pocock)

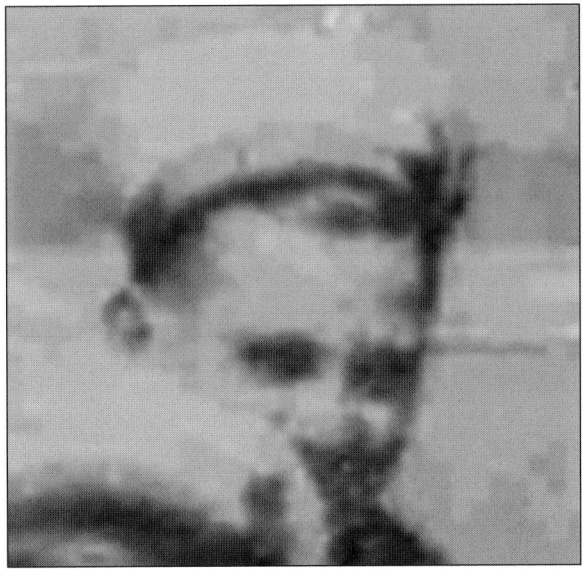

Amongst the Royal Marines lost with HMS *Royal Oak* was 18-year-old Marine Raymond Charles 'Charlie' Kane, the son of John and Elsie Kane of South Wigston, Leicestershire; he too remains missing and is commemorated on Panel 36, Column 1, of the Portsmouth Naval Memorial. (Katie Hobbs)

FACES OF HMS ROYAL OAK

Stoker 2nd Class James William Moar was an Orcadian, from Stromness, aged 19 when he went down with HMS *Royal Oak*; he is commemorated on Panel 35, Column 2, of the Portsmouth Naval Memorial. (Malcolm Norquay)

In Loving Memory
of
Our Dearly Beloved Son,
James Wm. Moar,
Stoker, 2nd Class, R.N.,
H.M.S. Royal Oak,
who died on war service
in Scapa Flow.
October 14th, 1939.
Aged 19 years.

Westside,
By Dounby,
Orkney.

Above and overleaf: The remembrance card commemorating Stoker Moar, shared with family and friends. (Malcolm Norquay)

Another Stoker 2nd Class, also aged 19, lost was George Charles Pollard, son of George and Sarah Pollard, of Eastbourne; he is commemorated on Panel 35, Column 2, of the Portsmouth Naval Memorial. (Anne Altomare)

P/KX 95936.
Y.C. Pollard Sto
Mess 56.
H.M.S. Royal Oak.
c/o G.P.O. London
E.C.I.

Sunday

My Dear Sister,
    Thanks alot for your letter, and I'am glad to say, that I'am still in the best of health, and smiling, but as you say it is hard to do so, some-times. Still sister it is all for a good cause.
    Well Win who is the new boy friend, you son of a gun. Still it is up to you, which one you want. By the way Win, Betty and I are still going a head with writting

Above, opposite and overleaf: Stoker Pollard's last letter home, written to his sister, 'Win', the Sunday before he sent down with his ship. (Anne Altomare)

to one another, believe me sister she is the one I want. Do me a good turn, and go up and see her one after-noon Win., may be go out with one another, as she as got the after-noon's off.

Dear sister I'am glad to hear that you are keeping Mum cheerful, as one don't know quite, whats going to happen next.

Wish Henry and Dorothy all the best for me Win, and as you say sister it was strange about my favourite being chosen like that, I thought it was going, during the week there.

Well Win I bet Sheila is having a good time now, with those

children down with her, as she still got that broken language, you know —? etc.

Well dear sister I think this is all for now, so I close with my love. Cherio and keep smiling.

Your ever-loving
Brother George.
xxxxx
xxxxx

P.S. Don't for-get to drop a line, when ever you can Sister.

FACES OF HMS ROYAL OAK

From Portchester, Hampshire, Petty Officer Stoker Robert Edwin Clarke was the son of Walter and Alice Clarke, and husband of Madge Clarke. A veteran of the First World War and approaching the end of a long period of service, Robert was 38 when he went down with HMS *Royal Oak*; remembered on Panel 35, Column 1, of the Portsmouth Naval Memorial. (Alex Murray)

FACES OF HMS ROYAL OAK

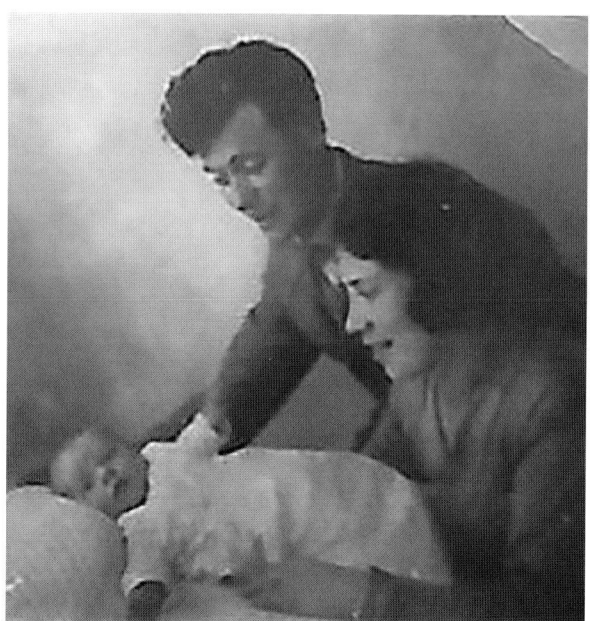

Able Seaman Frank Logan, of Portsmouth, was thirty-six when he lost his life aboard HMS *Royal Oak*, leaving behind a widow, Ivy. The couple are seen here in 1931 with their son, Michael. (Martin Barrett)

John Atkinson, from County Durham, preferred a life at sea to coal-mining, so became a Royal Marine. Married to Susannah, John settled in Gosport, the couple having a son, George, and daughter, Susan. John was thirty-nine when lost aboard HMS Royal Oak, and is commemorated on Panel 36, Column 1, of the Portsmouth Naval Memorial. (Carol Pardy)

FACES OF HMS ROYAL OAK

Leonard Cass pictured whilst training on HMS *Vincent*, aged sixteen. Two years later, in 1930, he signed on for twelve years and was a Leading Seaman when lost with HMS *Royal Oak* – remembered on Panel 33, Column 2, of the Portsmouth Naval Memorial. (Deborah Peach)

Leading Seaman Ronald Derbyshire was born on 3 May 1910 in landlocked Burton-on-Trent, Staffordshire, but from an early age yearned to go to sea. He joined the RN aged fifteen in 1925, training at HMS *Ganges*, later serving on HMS *London* and HMS *Hood*, on the latter winning silver oars as a rowing champion. Posted to HMS *Royal Oak* on 1 June 1939, he was twenty-nine when lost, leaving a widow, Edna, and two young sons. Ronald is remembered on Panel 33, Column 2, of the Portsmouth Naval Memorial; his grandson, Gareth Derbyshire, is Honorary Secretary of the HMS Royal Oak Association. This photograph is believed to have been taken aboard HMS *Hood*. (Gareth Derbyshire)

FACES OF HMS ROYAL OAK

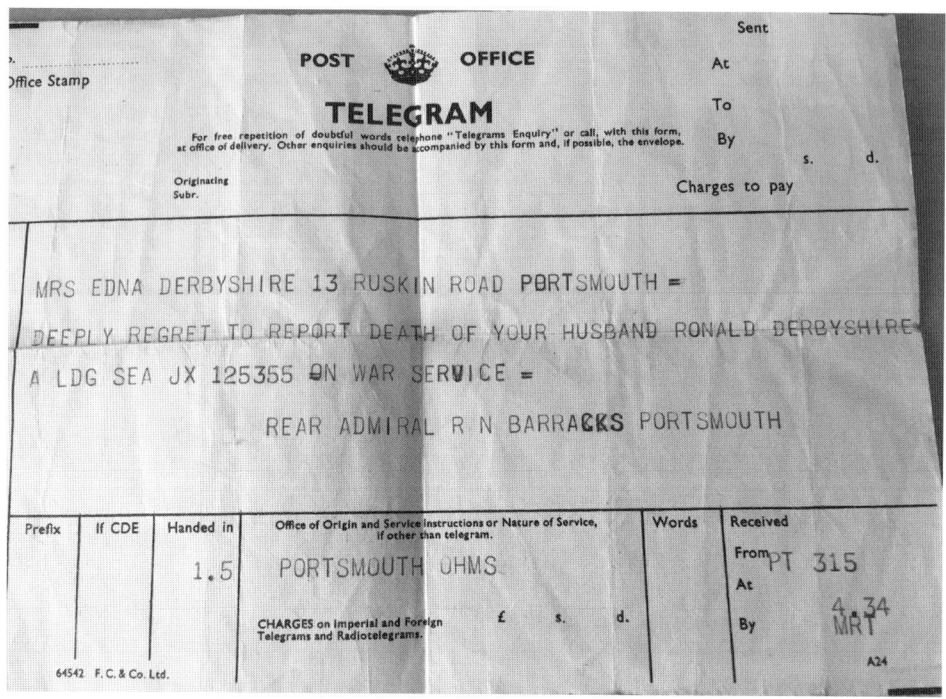

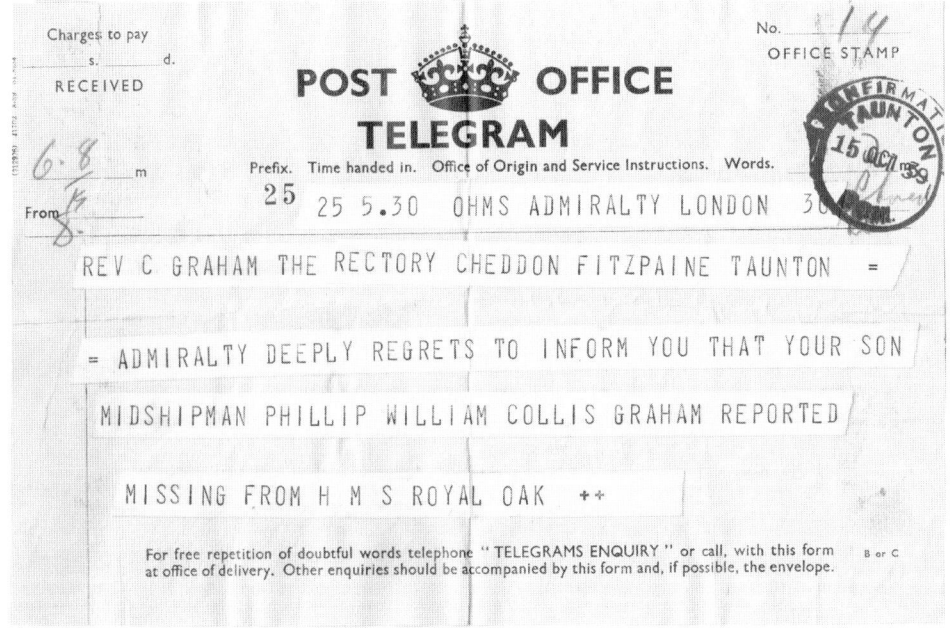

FACES OF HMS ROYAL OAK

C.W. 20121/39

17th October, 1939.

Reverend Sir,

In confirmation of Admiralty telegram of the 14th October, I am commanded by My Lords Commissioners of the Admiralty to state that they have been informed that your son, Midshipman Phillip William Colles Graham, Royal Navy, is presumed to have lost his life in the sinking of H.M.S. ROYAL OAK on 14th October.

My Lords desire to express to you their deep regret at receiving this intelligence and their profound sympathy in your great loss.

I am, Reverend Sir,

Your obedient Servant,

[signature]

The Rev. Christopher Graham,
The Rectory,
Cheddon,
Fitzpaine,
Taunton.

Above: The official Admiralty letter received by Midshipman Graham's father; he is remembered on Panel 33, Column 1, of the Portsmouth Naval Memorial. (Philip Marsden)

Opposite above: The telegram notifying Edna Derbyshire that her husband had lost his life on 14 October 1939. (Gareth Derbyshire)

Opposite below: Unfortunately, we have no photograph of Midshipman Philip WC Graham, he son of the Rev. Christopher and Mrs Graham of Cheddon Fitzpaine Rectory, Somerset. Philip was nineteen when reported missing that fateful night at Scapa Flow. This is the sad telegram that his parents received. (Philip Marsden)

FACES OF HMS ROYAL OAK

Above: A pre-war postcard of HMS *Royal Oak* from the Graham family archive. (Philip Marsden)

Left: Chief Electrical Artificer Herbert Mitchley Johns on the occasion of his marriage to Thora; he was thirty-seven when lost. (Julia Burgess)

FACES OF HMS ROYAL OAK

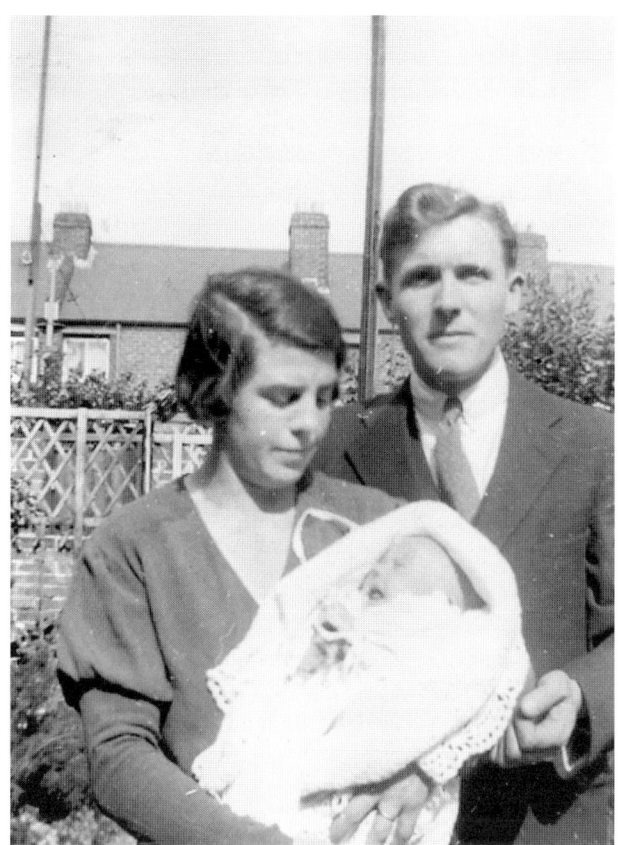

Herbert and Thora Johns with their first daughter in 1933; their second was born shortly after his death on 14 October 1939. Herbert is remembered on Panel 35, Column 3, of the Portsmouth Naval Memorial. (Julia Burgess)

Petty Officer (Supply) William Francis Kidby had married Alice Twelves, of Southsea, in 1931, and was thirty-four when lost aboard HMS *Royal Oak*; he is remembered on Panel 35, Column 3, of the Portsmouth Naval Memorial. (Eddie Kidby)

FACES OF HMS ROYAL OAK

Petty Officer George Oxley was a Londoner, from Kentish Town, seen here on the happy occasion of his marriage to Elizabeth – just two months before he too went down with HMS *Royal Oak*; he was twenty-eight and is remembered on Panel 33, Column 1, of the Portsmouth Naval Memorial. (Mark Newman)

Stoker Petty Officer Edward Robertson Peters had followed his father into the RN, serving on various ships, mainly in the Mediterranean Fleet, before a posting to HMS *Royal Oak* in July 1939. On Boxing Day 1930 he married Nelly Alexandra Edwards in Windsor, the couple ultimately buying a house in Portsmouth and having two children, Roy and Diane. Well-known throughout the RN as a gifted sportsman, Edward was thirty-two when lost and is remembered on Panel 35, Column 1, of the Portsmouth Naval Memorial. (Diane and Peter Bryant)

FACES OF HMS ROYAL OAK

Stoker Chief Petty Officer John William Welch, seen standing earlier in service, was a Petty Officer aboard HMS *Royal Oak*, and survived the sinking. In 1946, he left the RN after twenty-two-years' service and died in 1979, aged seventy-three. This is his account of 14 October 1939, as related to a family member:

> 'He was off duty that night and on deck having a cigarette when the ship shuddered, a small explosion. They didn't know what had happened and assumed they were safe within the Scapa Flow anchorage. Then, within seconds, the next torpedo hit they realised what it was. The ship started to list and he slid down the side into the water, but there was fire and his hands and face were burned. He was a strong swimmer, as he used to play water polo for the RN; whilst in the water he helped another man, keeping him afloat until they were picked up by the Daisy 2, but it wasn't until they were taken on board that he realised the other man had died. After that he spent some time in hospital and was then sent back to Portsmouth. He always said that if he had been in his bunk he wouldn't have survived.' (Mark Newman)

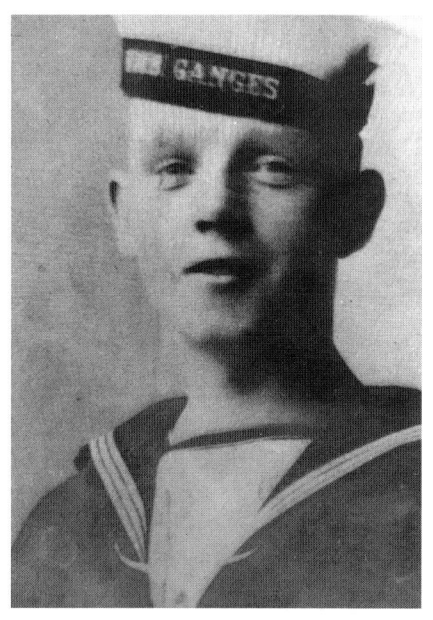

Left, below and opposite: Boy 1st Class Stanley Wood, from Liverpool, was only seventeen when lost with HMS Royal Oak. He was one of two boy sailors aboard of the same name. On 15 October 1939, Stanley's mother, Jane Wood, a widow, received a telegram confirming that their son had survived the tragedy. In a cruel twist of fate, this was an administrative error, and a follow-up telegram soon arrived announcing Stanley's death. In turmoil, the family sought urgent clarification from the Admiralty – but a third telegram left no doubt as to Stanley's fate. All three telegrams can be seen here. Stanley is commemorated on Panel 34, Column 3, of the Portsmouth Naval Memorial. (Val Farragher)

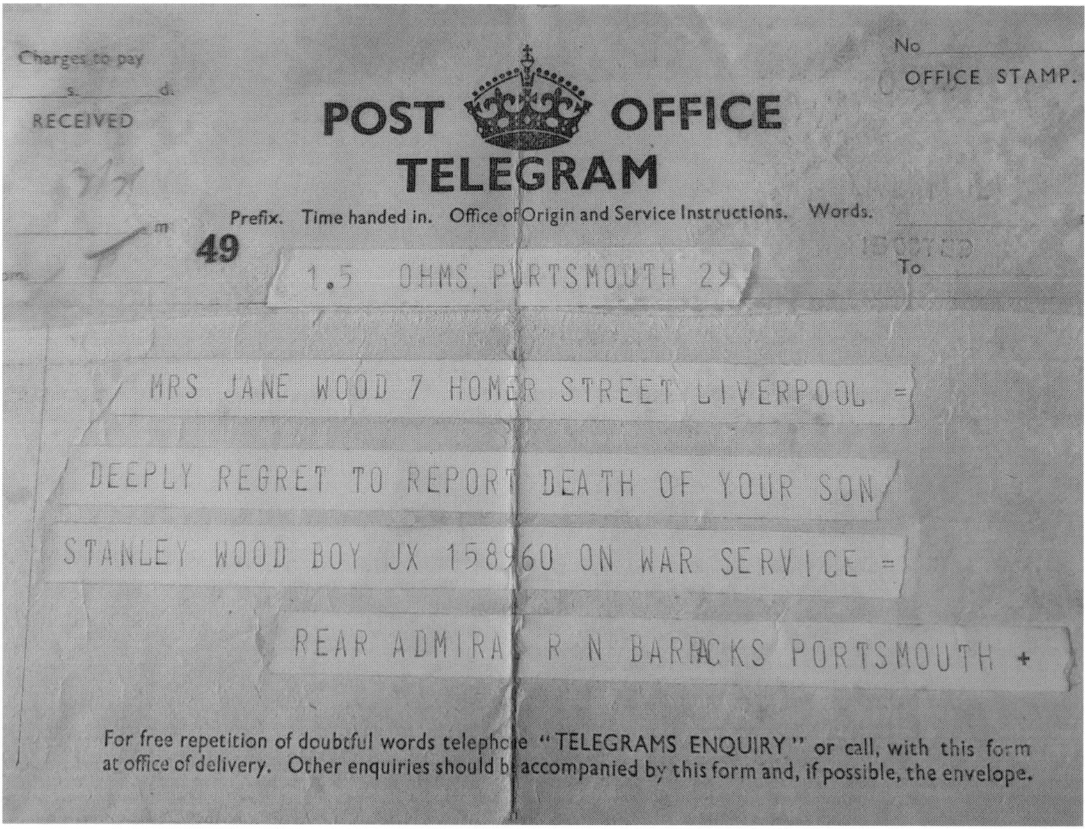

Charges to pay
s. d.
RECEIVED

No
OFFICE STAMP.

POST OFFICE
TELEGRAM

Prefix. Time handed in. Office of Origin and Service Instructions. Words.

49

1.5 OHMS PORTSMOUTH 29

To

MRS JANE WOOD 7 HOMER STREET LIVERPOOL =

DEEPLY REGRET TO REPORT DEATH OF YOUR SON

STANLEY WOOD BOY JX 158960 ON WAR SERVICE =

REAR ADMIRAL R N BARRACKS PORTSMOUTH +

For free repetition of doubtful words telephone "TELEGRAMS ENQUIRY" or call, with this form at office of delivery. Other enquiries should be accompanied by this form and, if possible, the envelope.

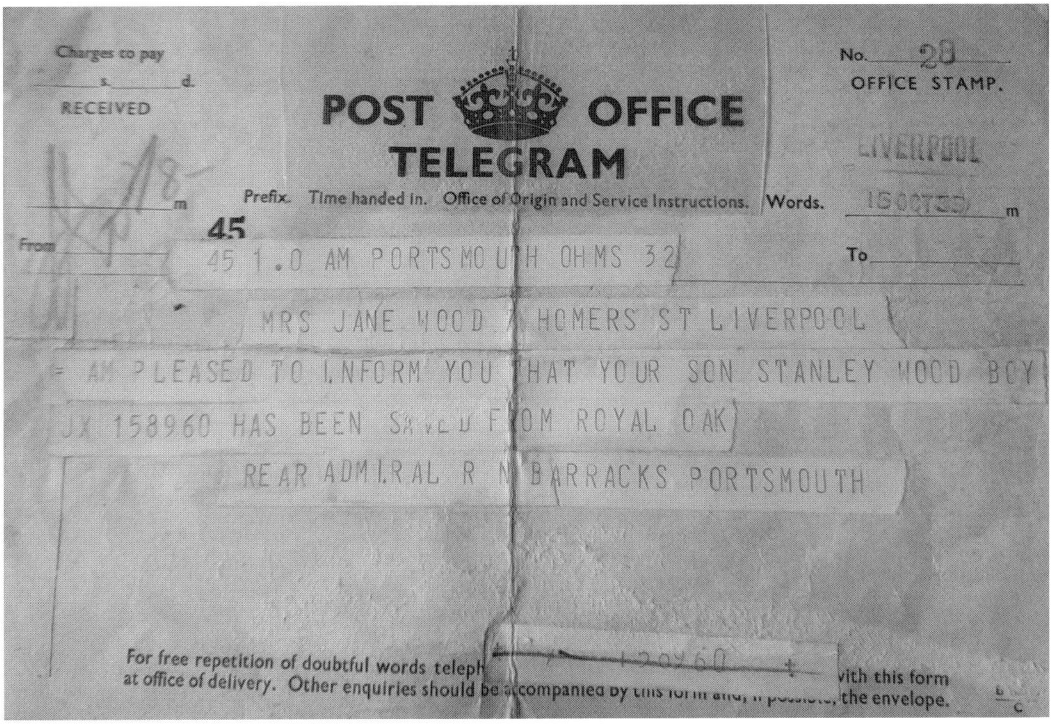

FACES OF HMS ROYAL OAK

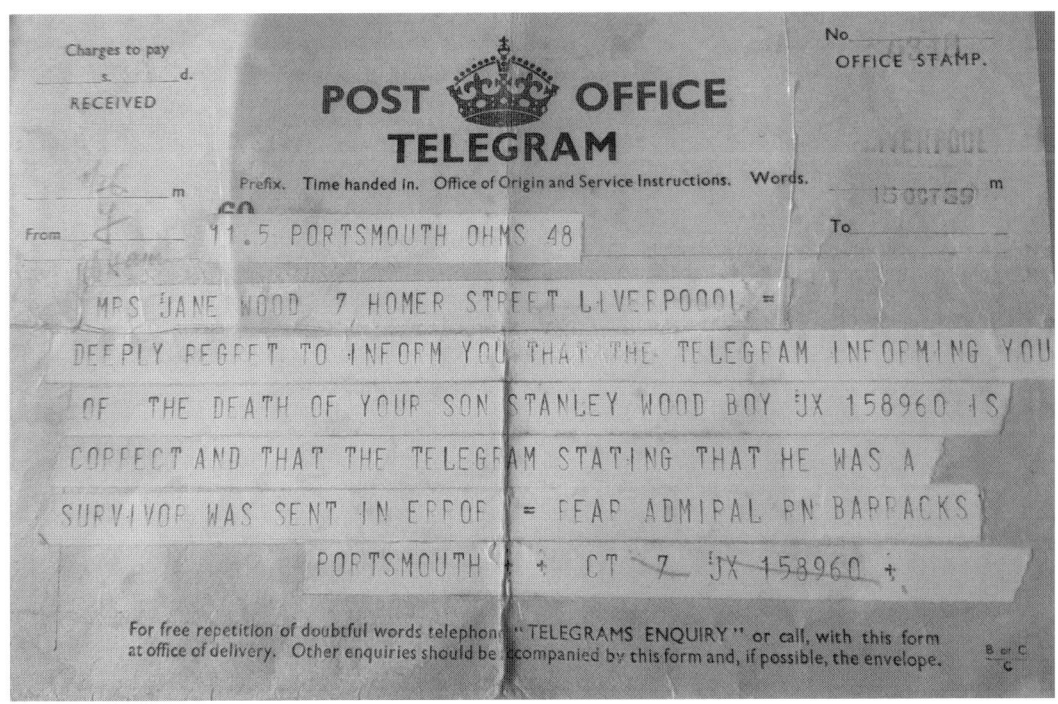

Petty Officer Henry Arthur Kersey was a 34-year-old gunner's mate with nineteen years' service when he went down with HMS *Royal Oak*. Pictured here with his wife, Violet, the family's home was in Hove, where Mrs Kersey was left a war widow with three boys to bring up. Petty Officer Kersey is remembered on Panel 33, Column 1, of the Portsmouth Naval Memorial. (Wally Kersey)

FACES OF HMS ROYAL OAK

The Manwaring brothers, from Fratton, Portsmouth: from left, Ordinary Seaman Douglas Manwaring and Stoker 1st Class William Richard Manwaring with their brother, Cyril. Both Douglas, 18, and Richard (by which name he was known), a married man of 27, were lost with HMS *Royal Oak*; they are remembered on Panel 34, Column 1, and Panel 35, Column 2, respectively, on the Portsmouth Naval Memorial. (Alan & Elaine Holloway)

FACES OF HMS ROYAL OAK

Leading Seaman Ernest Edgar Newnham joined as a boy sailor in 1924. When he went down with HMS *Royal Oak* he was 29 and married to Norma May Newnham, of Arlesford, Hampshire. He is remembered on Panel 33, Column 2, of the Portsmouth Naval Memorial. (Colin Barnard)

FACES OF HMS ROYAL OAK

Able Seaman Charles John Palmer was one of five brothers, from Laindon, Essex, and first of three to join the Royal Navy, in 1921 – he was also the first to die, on HMS *Royal Oak*, and is remembered on Panel 33, Column 3, of the Portsmouth Naval Memorial. On 9 May 1940, his brother, Leading Telegraphist Albert Palmer, was killed when HMS *Kelly* was damaged off Sylt by an E-Boat attack. Finally, Leading Seaman Edward Palmer went down with HMS *Fleur de Lys*, torpedoed by U-206 on 14 October 1941. (Mike Merrison)

ESSEX COUNTY CONSTABULARY.

FORM No. 101.

Brentwood Division.
Laindon Station.
15th. October, 1939.

TELEPHONE MESSAGE.

From Rear Admiral, R.N. Barracks, Portsmouth.
To Mrs. Jessie PALMER, "Lyndhurst", Wash Road, Laindon.

Despatched at ____ Received at ____
By ____ By ____

Deeply regret to report death of your son, Charles J. PALMER, Able Seaman No. J.101960, on War Service.

Above: The telegram received by Mrs Jessie Palmer informing her that the first of her three sons, all killed serving with the Royal Navy during the Second World War, had been lost with HMS *Royal Oak*, unusually sent via the local Constabulary. (Mike Merrison)

Left: From Portchester, Hampshire, Stoker 2nd Class Thomas George Osborne was 19 when lost with HMS *Royal Oak*; he is remembered on Panel 35, Column 2, of the Portsmouth Naval Memorial. (Kate Hooper)

FACES OF HMS ROYAL OAK

In 1938, Stoker 2nd Class Ernest Edward Perkins, a Londoner, joined the Royal Navy with his friend, Doug White, who survived the *Royal Oak* disaster. Ernest was seen alive in the water, having abandoned ship, but was not among those rescued and is remembered on Panel 35, Column 2, of the Portsmouth Naval Memorial. (H.A. Minors)

FACES OF HMS ROYAL OAK

Boy Bugler (Royal Marines) Aubrey John Priestley, from Slough, was among the youngest to die in Scapa Flow that fateful night, aged 15. His friend and fellow Boy Bugler Jim Sholl recalled: 'We were both fairly smart and one day were sent for by the Bugle Major who said that we had been chosen to be Easter Guards (while the rest were on leave) and after which we would go on the Royal Tour to the 1939 World Fair in America (on the escort ship HMS *Glasgow*). John took his best dress uniform home on our leave period for his mother to alter the collar, but, unfortunately, he lost it on the bus-journey so was unable to make it to the *Glasgow*. Instead, he was on the next draft to HMS *Royal Oak* and subsequently lost his life.' Abrey is remembered on Panel 36, Column 2, of the Portsmouth Naval Memorial. (Jim Sholl)

FACES OF HMS ROYAL OAK

Leading Seaman Lesley George Squires, from Bournemouth, had joined the Royal Navy in 1924, having previously worked as a bank clerk, and was an experienced seaman when he lost his life in Scapa Flow. Married to Nellie, the couple had a 15-month-old baby, Robert, when Lesley was reported missing; he is remembered on Panel 33, Column 2, of the Portsmouth Naval Memorial. (Robert Squires)

FACES OF HMS ROYAL OAK

Chief Petty Officer Cook William Small, from Southampton, and married to Ivy, was survived by his wife, two sons (aged 8 and 5), and his 4-year-old daughter; he is remembered on Panel 35, Column 3, of the Portsmouth Naval Memorial. (Keith Small)

17-year-old Boy 1st Class Harry, from Mexborough, Yorkshire, was a gunner; remembered on Panel 34, Column 2, of the Portsmouth Naval Memorial. (Mr & Mrs A Gamble)

```
Charges to pay
  s.      d.
RECEIVED

                    TELEGRAM

Prefix.  Time handed In.  Office of Origin and Service Instructions.  Words.

  84    1.5 PORTSMOUTH T OHMS 29

MRS EMMA SPENCER 26 BRYDEN RD MEXBOROUGH YORKS =

DEEPLY REGRET TO REPORT DEATH OF YOUR SON HARRY SPENCER
BOY JX 158255 ON WAR SERVICE =

= REAR ADMIRAL R N BARRACKS PORTSMOUTH +
```

No. 0047 — OFFICE STAMP SHEFFIELD 16 OCT 39

JX 158255

The telegram reporting Harry Spencer's death. (Mr and Mrs A Gamble)

Opposite: Assistant Cook Mark Warren Stephens was born in Southampton on 22 September 1917, a month after his merchant sailor father's death on the ammunition ship SS *Wisbech*. Before the war, Mark served aboard the Royal Mail Line's *Alacantra*, and transferred to the Royal Navy when war broke out. He too was lost with HMS *Royal Oak* and is remembered on Panel 35, Column 3, of the Portsmouth Naval Memorial. (Via Sara Frith)

FACES OF HMS ROYAL OAK

FACES OF HMS ROYAL OAK

Left: From Liphook in Hampshire, Stoker 2nd Class Leonard George Trussler was 19 when lost with HMS *Royal Oak* and is remembered on Panel, 35 Column 2, of the Portsmouth Naval Memorial. (Kay Howarth)

Below: William Gemmell Mitchell 'Willie' Baker was an Orcadian, from Stromness, seen here on the cannon at Guardhouse Lookout, Stromness, looking out across the Flow and dreaming of achieving his ambition of a life at sea. (Colin Gray)

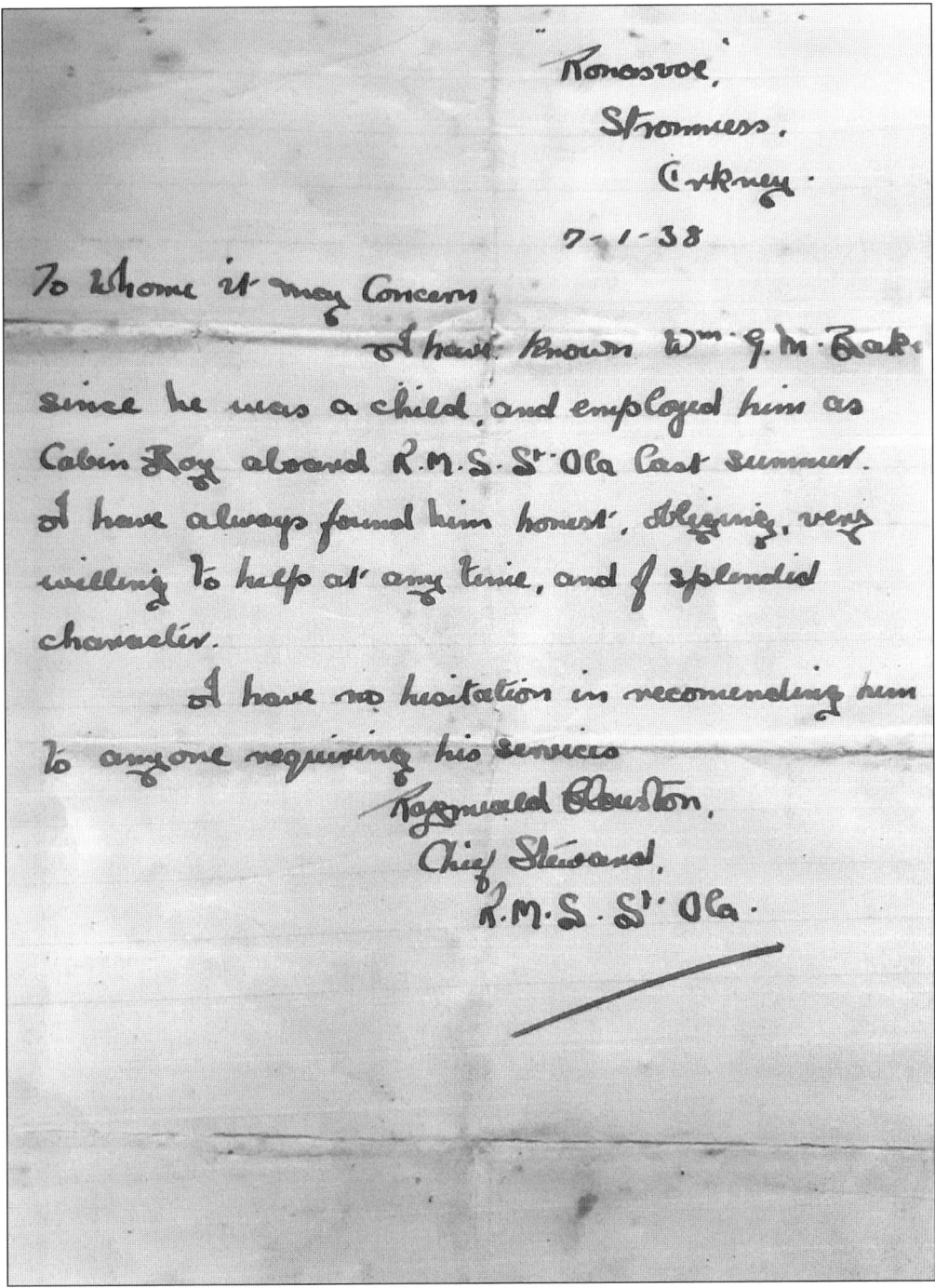

Willie Baker first went to sea after leaving school as a cabin boy on the RMS *St Ola*, before joining the Royal Navy; this is the reference supporting his application. (Colin Gray)

FACES OF HMS ROYAL OAK

Excited and proud to be anchored in Scapa Flow so close to his home town, sadly Boy 1st Class W.G.M. Baker would go down with HMS *Royal Oak*, aged 16. He is remembered on Panel 34, Column 1, of the Portsmouth Naval Memorial. (Colin Gray)

FACES OF HMS ROYAL OAK

From Wantage, Berkshire, the son of a Master Confectioner, Able Seaman Joseph Pascal Wilkins joined the Royal Navy as a boy in 1921, having previously served in the Mercantile Marine. Joseph is seen here with his wife, Ada, of North End, Portsmouth; the couple had three children, two boys and a girl. (Bryan Wilkins)

FACES OF HMS ROYAL OAK

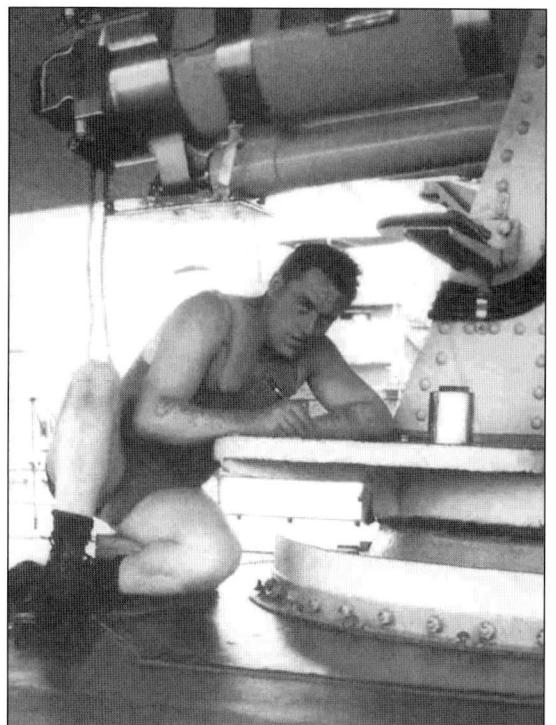

Left: Able Seaman J.P. Wilkins was an experienced seaman and 36 when lost with HMS *Royal Oak*, on which ship he is seen here, writing home. He is remembered on Panel 33, Column 3, of the Portsmouth Naval Memorial. (Bryan Wilkins)

Below, opposite and overleaf: It is believed that 1,259 sailors were aboard HMS *Royal Oak* on the fateful night, only 424 of whom survived; 835 souls were lost. Of these casualties, only twenty-six were recovered from the sea, all of whom were buried at Lyness Royal Naval Cemetery on the Orkney island of Hoy – eight of them unidentified. These photographs show the military funeral for the *Royal Oak* casualties at Lyness, the survivors marching behind the guard of honour. (Orkney Library & Archive)

FACES OF HMS ROYAL OAK

FACES OF HMS ROYAL OAK

FACES OF HMS ROYAL OAK

Above: The *Royal Oak* graves pictured today at the Lyness Royal Naval Cemetery, immaculately maintained by the Commonwealth War Graves Commission.

Right: The original grave markers at Lyness. (Pat Johnson)

FACES OF HMS ROYAL OAK

The funeral, with full military honours, was led by the Rev. John Scarff, who became a family friend of Ordinary Telegraphist Thomas W Jackson, whose grave can be seen on the right in the preceding picture. Thomas's father, also Thomas Jackson, would send roses from his garden in Houghton-le-Spring, County Durham, for the kindly cleric to place on his sailor son's grave. (Pat Johnson)

FACES OF HMS ROYAL OAK

Ordinary Telegraphist Thomas W Jackson, who was nineteen when lost with HMS *Royal Oak*. (Pat Johnson)

Thomas Jackson's grave at Lyness today, the original metal marker having long since been replaced by the usual headstone. (Pat Johnson)

FACES OF HMS ROYAL OAK

Also amongst the dead that fateful night of 14 October 1939 was Electrical Artificer First Class Charles E Benney, who was thirty-seven. Married to Vera, the couple's home was in Southwick, Sussex. (Sheila West)

Charles Benney's grave at Lyness. After the death of his widow, Vera, in 2005, her ashes were partially interred with Charles, with the blessing of the Commonwealth War Graves Commission, an undertaking which was a deeply moving and personal pilgrimage for Charles and Vera's daughter, Shelia West and her son, Graham. (Sheila West)

Stoker First Class Victor George Wren was a 39-year-old married man from Portland, Dorset, with two sons when lost; his remains were recovered and interred at Lyness. (Mrs J. Mason)

Stoker Wren's grave at Lyness.

FACES OF HMS ROYAL OAK

Chief Stoker Jonah Williams, a 38-year-old married Yorkshireman, also lost his life and was among those casualties recovered from the sea. (Michelle Hare)

Chief Stoker Williams' grave at Lyness – he was identified by one of his tattoos.

The grave of an unidentified *Royal Oak* casualty at Lyness – around 800 of the crew were never found.

FACES OF HMS ROYAL OAK

Among the survivors was Royal Marine Sergeant John Joseph Coombes, known to all as 'Ian'. Married to Dorothy, with a daughter and a son, she remembered that after returning home to Sheet, her 26-year-old husband 'was a changed man for a while'. Sadly, Ian was killed in May 1941, when being evacuated from Crete to Alexandria aboard HMS *Hereward*, which received a direct hit. (Dorothy Coombes)

Opposite: Also among the lucky survivors was Alfred Ronald Jordan, a Royal Marine from Corby, pictured here on HMS *Royal Oak*'s 'Right gun, 15-inch, A Turret', shortly before the sinking. other ships, including HMS *Iron Duke*, went on to enjoy a long career in the service, eventually retiring in 1957. (Chris Jordan)

FACES OF HMS ROYAL OAK

FACES OF HMS ROYAL OAK

Survivor Marine Jordan, 'Scapa Flow, Kirkwall end', 27 August 1939. (Chris Jordan)

One of the lucky ones was Boy 1st Class Bert Pocock, a 'Reading townie', who survived the sinking and later served on HMS *Manchester*, surviving the war.

FACES OF HMS ROYAL OAK

Survivor Bert Pocock at the 2004 HMS *Royal Oak* Association's commemorative service at the Portsmouth Naval Memorial at Southsea.

Royal Marine Musician Alf Fordham also survived – but only narrowly, given that a white-hot flame missed him by inches when the cordite magazine exploded.

Alf Fordham survived the war and remained devoted to remembering his fallen comrades at every opportunity.

FACES OF HMS ROYAL OAK

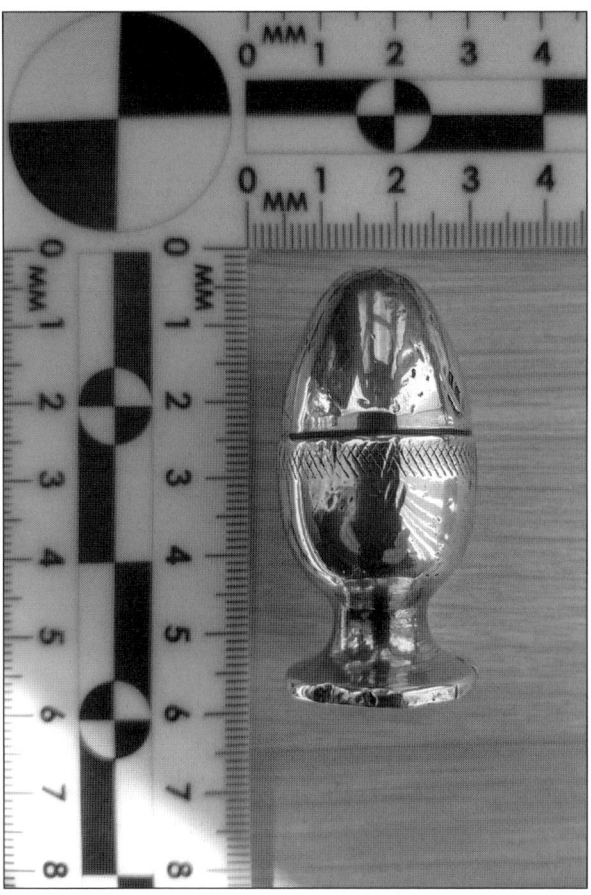

When based at Scapa Flow in 1939 aboard HMS *Glasgow*, Petty Officer Stoker John Wotherspoon 'acquired' this acorn, apparently a locker or drawer handle from the officers' quarters of HMS *Royal Oak*, which he brought home to Gosport when on home leave. (Nick Wotherspoon)

Thirty-two-year old Petty Officer Stoker John Wotherspoon, who 'acquired' the acorn from HMS *Royal Oak*. In November 1939, Wotherspoon joined the destroyer HMS *Glowworm* but lost his life on 8 April 1940 when his ship was sunk off Norway in an epic action against the German heavy cruiser *Admiral Hipper*; he is commemorated on Panel 41, Column 3, of the Portsmouth Naval Memorial. (Nick Wotherspoon)

FACES OF HMS ROYAL OAK

Boy 1st Class Kenneth Toop also survived. According to post-war research by Kenneth, there were 163 Boy Seamen, Boy Telegraphists and Boy Signalmen aboard HMS *Royal Oak* when the ship was attacked by U-47 – only 37 were saved.

For many years the now late Kenneth Toop was the tireless honorary secretary of the HMS *Royal Oak* Association, pictured here at the 2004 Southsea service.

The 2004 HMS *Royal Oak* service being presided over by the Revd Ron Patterson MBE, who served on HMS *Hood* between the wars.

FACES OF HMS ROYAL OAK

Ron Patterson when a Boy 1st Class aboard HMS *Hood*.

Mrs Kate Hooper remembering her brother, Stoker Tom Osborne, at the Portsmouth Naval Memorial.

FACES OF HMS ROYAL OAK

Similarly, Paul Humber remembering his brother, Boy 1st Class John Francis Humber.

Opposite: The Portsmouth Naval Memorial on Southsea Common, on which the vast majority of HMS *Royal Oak*'s crew are commemorated. Indeed, some 25,000 sailors of both world wars who have no known grave are remembered here.

On Orkney, the tragedy remains well-remembered and commemorated. This is the recovered ship's bell displayed in St Magnus Cathedral, Kirkwall, as a memorial to those who died. Below is the Book of Remembrance, recording names of the dead.

Although since The Protection of Military Remains Act 1986, the wreck-site of HMS *Royal Oak* has been a protected war grave, on which recreational diving is prohibited, some years beforehand a 'wrecker' recovered the brass letters spelling the ship's name – since donated to the Scapa Flow Visitor Centre at Lyness.

FACES OF HMS ROYAL OAK

The plaque accompanying the oak tree planted to remember HMS *Royal Oak* at The National Memorial Arboretum, Alrewas, Staffordshire.

The buoy marking the wreck site of HMS *Royal Oak* – only about a mile offshore.

The wreck-site marker festooned with wreaths and flowers.

FACES OF HMS ROYAL OAK

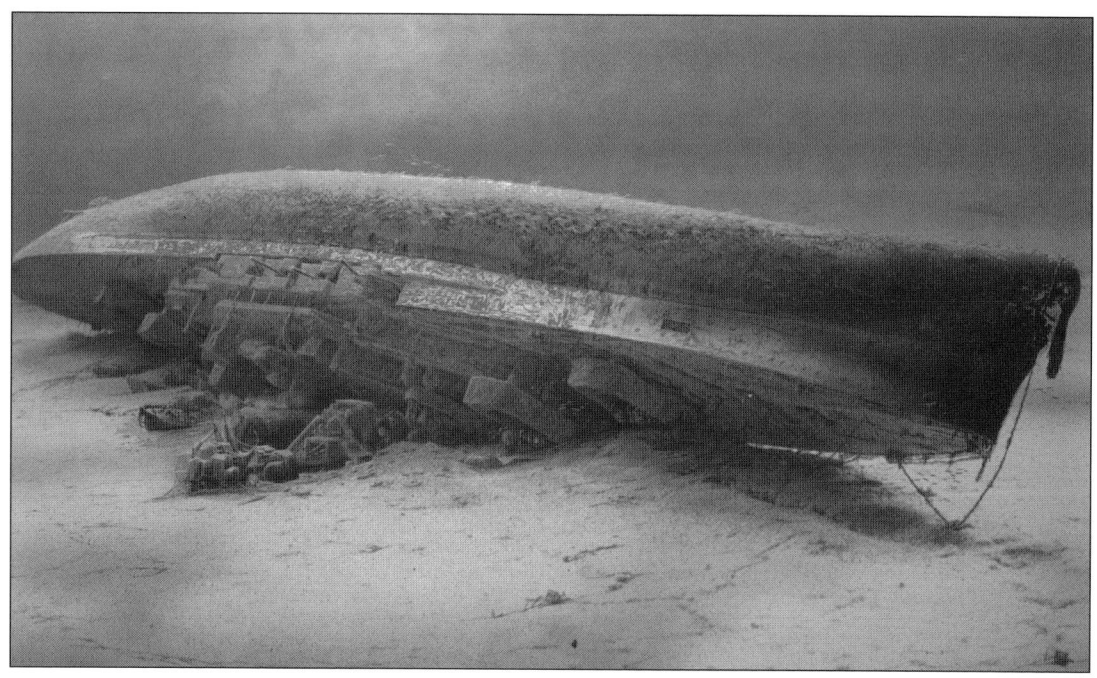

Above: An excellent artist's impression of how the wreck appears today. (Peter Rowlands, Ocean Optics)

Left: Annually, Royal Navy divers descend on the wreck to replace the white ensign on HMS *Royal Oak*. Perhaps appropriately, the wreck is covered in soft corals known as 'dead man's fingers'.

On 14 October 2019, the memorial erected by survivors, families and friends of The *Royal Oak* Association, together with Orkney Islands Council, was unveiled on the sinking's eightieth anniversary. The obelisk can be seen in the Royal Oak Remembrance Garden at Scapa Beach. Annually, services commemorating the HMS *Royal Oak* tragedy are held on Orkney, Portsmouth, and elsewhere. Gone she and her gallant company are – but certainly not forgotten.

FACES OF HMS ROYAL OAK

Remarkably, a member of U-47's crew, Herbert Hermann, a torpedo mechanic on the Scapa Flow mission, became a friend of the HMS Royal Oak Association and attended many annual commemorations. On 14 October 1967, Hermann, together with three other U-47 survivors, laid a wreath at the annual commemoration in Portsmouth, beginning a process of reconciliation and healing. Ultimately, U-47 was lost with all hands, but fortunately for some of the crew who had been on the Scapa Flow sortie they had been posted beforehand to other boats or duties. Hermann, served on several other boats, for example, until U-1209 ran aground off the Cornish coast in 1944. The crew were captured and Hermann was first held in a camp near Lockerbie, marrying a local girl and making Scotland his permanent post-war home. Hermann is pictured here (left) with a *Royal Oak* survivor, Norman 'Taff' Davies, before casting a wreath over the wreck site. (Orkney Library & Archive)

FACES OF HMS ROYAL OAK

The mighty HMS *Royal Oak* as she is best remembered – firing a broadside during gunnery practice off the Old Man of Hoy. (Orkney Library & Archive)

Acknowledgements

Many years ago, whist on an expedition to dive the German High Seas Fleet wrecks at Scapa Flow, Bob Anderson, Skipper of MV Halton, motored between dives one day to show me the wreck-site marker of HMS *Royal Oak*. Being well-aware of the tragedy I was deeply moved to see the flowers, wreaths and notes wired to the buoy by family and friends of those lost – so began researching the story from the hidden perspective of the actual crew. That led to publication of my original book, *Hearts of Oak*, in which endeavor I was enormously encouraged and assisted by Kenneth Toop, a survivor of the sinking and tireless honorary secretary of the HMS Royal Oak Association. Fellow historian Peter Rowlands was also very helpful, so arguably without Bob, Kenneth and Peter, neither *Hearts of Oak* or this book would exist.

Thanks to the internet, research is infinitely easier today, in terms of checking facts, making contacts, undertaking genealogical research and appealing for information. Indeed, for this book I am indebted to the HMS Royal Oak Association, and in particular the Honorary Secretary, Gareth Derbyshire, who also kindly contributed the foreword; 'HMS Royal Oak Families & Friends' Facebook page, Mick Fisher, Orkney Library & Archive, and Ian Sayer.

As ever, Martin Mace, Amy Jordan, and the team at Pen & Sword were a pleasure to work with.

Last, but certainly not least, the following relatives and friends of HMS *Royal Oak's* ship's company who have so kindly contributed information and photographs:

> Linda Warren (PO HG Attfield); Margaret Hothi (PO FC Bealing); Mick Fisher (LS JB Fisher); AS TH Chadwick (Steven W Chadwick); Paul Clacher (Boy 1st Class WH Clacher); Conway-

FACES OF HMS ROYAL OAK

Hughes (Paymaster Captain J Cundall Cherry); Jean Westerman (PO V Cruse); OS C Heslop (Susan Heslop); Graham Farr (CS EW Farr); Roy Ingham (LS HS Huggins); Jim Perkins (Stoker E Perkins); Peter Gisborne (CPO F Rann); Mary Cole (AS S Cole); Ralph Cousins (SA HJ Cousins); Gordon Stoker (Boy 1st Class F Marshall); Juie Bisson (Boy 1st Class D Patch); Steve Wales (PO WD Royal); Kieran Ellix (Boy 1st Class EW Scovell); Tania Bolton (Marine VLJ Pierpoint); Leading Stoker F Walker and WJ Hawkins); Malcolm Warriner (Leading Seaman EB Warriner); Tony Royal Wormald (Able Seaman James Lawrence Wormald); Doris Leek (Boy 1st Class Roland Arno); Margaret Warburton (SA AE Bargery); Rachel Chesman (LS WE Chesman); Joan Hathaway (Boy 1st Class H Griffin); Brian Otway (Bandmaster A Golding); Shirley Bird (Marine KE Hall); Kathryn Trower (Marine CF Hemsley); Paul Humber (Boy 1st Class JF Humber); Wally Kersey (PO HA Kersey); Alan and Elaine Holloway (OS D Manwaring and Stoker 1st Class WR Manwaring); Colin Barnard (LS EE Newnham); Mike Merrison (AS CJ Palmer); Kate Hooper (Stoker TG Osborne); HA Minors (Stoker EE Perkins); Jim Sholl (Boy Bugler (RM) AJ Priestley); Robert Squires (LS LG Squires); Keith Small (CPO W Small); Mr and Mrs A Gamble (Boy 1st Class H Spencer); Sara Frith (AC MW Stephens); Kay Howarth (Stoker LG Trussler); Colin Gray (Boy 1st Class WGM Baker); Bryan Wilkins (AS JP Wilkins); Mrs J Mason (Stoker VG Wren); Michelle Hare (CS J Williams); Alex Murray (CPO Stoker RE Clarke); Chris Jordan (RM AR Jordan); Carol Pardy (RM J Atkinson); Deborah Peach (LS L Cass); Gareth Derbyshire (LS R Derbyshire); Philip Marsden (Midshipman PWC Graham); Julia Burgess (CEA HM Johns); Eddie Kidby (PO WF Kidby); Mark Newman (PO GR Oxley and Stoker CPO JW Welch); Diane and Peter Bryant (Stoker PO ER Peters); Val Farragher (Boy 1st Class S Wood); Pat Johnson (OT TW Jackson); Sheila West (EA 1st Class CE Benney); Katie Hobbs (Marine RC Kane); Malcolm Norquay (Stoker JW Moar); Anne Altomare (Stoker GC Pollard); Martin Barrett (AS F Logan).

Bibliography

Primary Sources

Author's personal correspondence and interviews with veterans and the relatives of casualties.

Secondary Sources

Bekker, C., *Hitler's Naval War*, Corgi, London, 1976
Brown, M. & Meehan, P., *Scapa Flow: The Story of Britain's Greatest Naval Anchorage in the Two World Wars*, The Penguin Press, London, 1968
Frank, W., *Enemy Submarine*, William Kimber & Co Ltd, London, 1954
Mallman Showell, J., *German Navy Handbook 1939-45*, Sutton Publishing, Stroud, 1999
Martindale, D., *Günther Prien and U-47: The Bull of Scapa Flow*, Pen & Sword, Barnsley, 2018
McKee, A., *Black Saturday*, first edition, Souvenir Press, London, 1966
Miller, J., *Scapa*, Berlinn Ltd, London, 2000
Prien, G., *U-boat Commander*, Tempus Publishing, Stroud, 2000
Rössler, E., *The U-Boat: The Evolution & Technical History of German Submarines*, Arms & Armour Press, London, 1981
Sharpe, P., *U-boat Fact File: Detailed Service Histories of the Submarines Operated by the* Kriegsmarine*, 1939-45*, Midland Publishing, Hinckley, 1998
Smith, P.L., *The Naval Wrecks of Scapa Flow*, The Orkney Press, Kirkwall, 1989

Stern, R.C., *Type VII U-boats*, Arms & Armour Press, London, 1981

Turton, E., Fitzsimmons, C., Rowland, C., Crofts, D., Kay, S., Hyttinen, K., Tynkkynen, M., & Wade, B. (2021). *HMS Royal Oak 80 Survey (2018-2019)*. University of Dundee. https://doi.org/10.20933/100001184

Weaver, H.J., *Nightmare at Scapa Flow: The Truth About the Sinking of HMS Royal Oak,* Cressrelles Publishing Co Ltd, Malvern, 1980

Williams, A., *The Battle of the Atlantic*, BBC Worldwide Ltd, London, 2002

Williamson., W, *Knights of the Iron Cross, 1939-45*, Blandford Press, London, 1987

Wood, L., *The Bull & the Barriers: The Wrecks of Scapa Flow*, Tempus Publishing, Stroud, 2000

Internet resources

www.hmsroyaloak.co.uk	Peter Rowlands' excellent site about the ship.
www.U47.org	Rick Joshua's site dedicated to U-47.
www.u-boat.net	The oracle of all U-boat sites.
www.cwgc.org	The Commonwealth War Grave Commissions' site featuring an essential casualty search facility.

Programmes

For an impression of life aboard a U-boat on an operational patrol, see Wolfgang Petersen's *Das Boot*, based upon the factual novel of that name by war correspondent Lothar-Günther Bucheim.

The documentary made by Peter Rowlands about HMS *Royal Oak*, which includes underwater footage of the wreck, is excellent and available from Submerged Publications, 5 Western College Road, Mannarmead, Plymouth PL4 7AG.

Fallen Oak: Revealing the Wreck of HMS Royal Oak. Incredible documentary made during the *Royal Oak 80 Survey*, which can be accessed at: https://vimeo.com/460447596/559fe3e0cc?fbclid=IwAR0r7YilejGx6WA4-LaUPY2lxoX9aeM-2OwrkJUn57u0xZc-ekIYSN9OmlI

Other Books by Dilip Sarkar

Spitfire Squadron: No 19 Squadron at War, 1939-41
The Invisible Thread: A Spitfire's Tale
Through Peril to the Stars: RAF Fighter Pilots Who Failed to Return, 1939-45
Angriff Westland: Three Battle of Britain Air Raids Through the Looking Glass
A Few of the Many: Air War 1939-45, A Kaleidoscope of Memories
Bader's Tangmere Spitfires: The Untold Story, 1941
Bader's Duxford Fighters: The Big Wing Controversy
Missing in Action: Resting in Peace?
Guards VC: Blitzkrieg 1940
Battle of Britain: The Photographic Kaleidoscope, Volumes I-IV
Fighter Pilot: The Photographic Kaleidoscope
Group Captain Sir Douglas Bader: An Inspiration in Photographs
Johnnie Johnson: Spitfire Top Gun, Part I
Johnnie Johnson: Spitfire Top Gun, Part II
Battle of Britain: Last Look Back
Spitfire! Courage & Sacrifice
Spitfire Voices: Heroes Remember
The Battle of Powick Bridge: Ambush a Fore-thought
Duxford 1940: A Battle of Britain Base at War
The Few: The Battle of Britain in the Words of the Pilots

FACES OF HMS ROYAL OAK

Spitfire Manual 1940

The Sinking of HMS Royal Oak In the Words of the Survivors (re-print of Hearts of Oak)

The Last of the Few: Eighteen Battle of Britain Pilots Tell Their Extraordinary Stories

Hearts of Oak: The Human Tragedy of HMS Royal Oak

Spitfire Voices: Life as a Spitfire Pilot in the Words of the Veterans

How the Spitfire Won the Battle of Britain

Spitfire Ace of Aces: The True Wartime Story of Johnnie Johnson

Douglas Bader

Fighter Ace: The Extraordinary Life of Douglas Bader, Battle of Britain Hero (re-print of above)

Spitfire: The Photographic Biography

Hurricane Manual 1940

River Pike

The Final Few: The Last Surviving Pilots of the Battle of Britain Tell Their Stories

Arnhem 1944: The Human Tragedy of the Bridge Too Far

Spitfire! The Full Story of a Unique Battle of Britain Fighter Squadron

Battle of Britain 1940: The Finest Hour's Human Cost

Letters from The Few: Unique Memories of the Battle of Britain

Johnnie Johnson's 1942 Diary: The War Diary of the Spitfire Ace of Aces

Johnnie Johnson's Great Adventure: The Spitfire Ace of Ace's Last Look Back

Sailor Malan – Freedom Fighter: The Inspirational Story of a Spitfire Ace

Spitfire Ace of Aces – The Album: The Photographs of Johnnie Johnson

The Real Spitfire Pilot

The Real Hurricane Pilot

Bader's Big Wing Controversy: Duxford 1940

Bader's Spitfire Wing: Tangmere 1941

FACES OF HMS ROYAL OAK

Spitfire Down

Forgotten Heroes of The Battle of Britain

Faces of The Few

Spitfire Faces

Arise to Conquer: The Real Hurricane Pilot (introduction, commentary and photographs supplied to a new edition of Wing Commander IR Gleed DSO DFC's wartime memoir)

Free French Spitfire Hero: The Diaries of and Search for René Mouchotte (with Jan Leeming)

The Battle of Britain on the Big Screen: 'The Finest Hour' Through British Cinema

Battle of Britain: The Movie (contributor to and publisher of the now late Robert Rudhall's original edition (2000), and editor and substantial contributor to 2022 revised edition)

Battle of Britain The Gathering Storm: Prelude to the Spitfire Summer of 1940

Battle of Britain The Breaking Storm: 10 July 1940 – 12 August 1940